The Q Guide

to Classic

Monster Movies

The Q Guides

FROM ALYSON BOOKS

POP CULTURE

Q GUIDE

OUT THERE

The Q Guide

to Classic

Monster Movies

Stuff You Didn't Even Know You Wanted to Know . . . about Dracula, the Mummy, and other Scary Creatures

[Douglas McEwan]

alyson books
NEW YORK

© 2007 BY DOUGLAS MCEWAN
ALL RIGHTS RESERVED

MANUFACTURED IN THE UNITED STATES OF AMERICA

THIS TRADE PAPERBACK ORIGINAL IS PUBLISHED BY
ALYSON BOOKS
245 WEST 17TH STREET,
NEW YORK, NY 10011

DISTRIBUTION IN THE UNITED KINGDOM BY
TURNAROUND PUBLISHER SERVICES LTD.
UNIT 3, OLYMPIA TRADING ESTATE
COBURG ROAD, WOOD GREEN,
LONDON N22 6TZ ENGLAND

FIRST EDITION: SEPTEMBER 2007

07 08 09 10 11 [a] 10 9 8 7 6 5 4 3 2 1

ISBN: 1-59350-006-8
ISBN-13: 978-1-59350-006-1

LIBRARY OF CONGRESS
CATALOGING-IN-PUBLICATION DATA ARE ON FILE.

COVER DESIGN BY VICTOR MINGOVITS

Jerry Vance was born in Boston in 1924. Early in his career he adopted the name Larry Vincent, but when he died all too young at fifty, in 1975, he was best known as "*Seymour,* The Master of the Macabre, The Epitome of Evil, The Most Sinister Man to Crawl Across the Face of the Earth." And "The Best TV Horror Host" that ever was. He was also the first person to pay me to write jokes about horror movies, and he was my friend. I miss him still, and I dedicate this book to his memory.

QUOTE

"There are far worse things awaiting man than death."
—Count Dracula (Bela Lugosi), *Dracula*

"To a new world of gods and monsters."
—Dr. Septimus Pretorius (Ernest Thesiger), *Bride of Frankenstein*

"This is no life for murderers."
—Karl (Dwight Frye), *Bride of Frankenstein*

"Just as soon as his problem's solved, he'll be as gay as a lark again. He's like that."
—Elsa Frankenstein (Josephine Hutchinson), *Son of Frankenstein*

"Nicki, your eyes! I've never seen them look so queer."
—John Ainsley (Roland Varno), *The Return of the Vampire*

"For life is short, but death is long. Faro la, faro li."
—Big Cheesy Gypsy Singer (Adia Kuznetzoff), *Frankenstein Meets the Wolfman*

"Aaaaaaaaaaaaaaaaaaaaahhh-hhhh!!!"
—Someone in every one of these movies

Contents

Introduction

Pardon Me, Boys, Is This the Transylvania Station?

> "It is one of the strangest tales ever told. It deals with the two great mysteries of creation, Life and Death. I think it will thrill you. It may shock you. It might even horrify you. So if any of you feel that you do not care to subject your nerves to such a strain, now's your chance to—uh—well, we warned you."

IT WAS A SATURDAY AFTERNOON IN 1962. I was twelve years old and standing at the magazine rack of the Mayfair Market in Redondo Beach, California, staring, transfixed, at a magazine cover showing a handsome man in a tuxedo and cape staring back at me. The man was Christopher Lee playing Count Dracula, and he held me captivated. I bought the magazine, and began a love affair that continues to this day.

As the years passed, growing up gay—and thus, by definition, an outsider, a "monster"—I felt a deep sense of connection to Dr. Henry Jekyll and Lawrence Talbot and Count Vlad Dracula and Baron sometimes-Henry-sometimes-Victor Frankenstein and even King Kong.

Dracula wasn't gay, though in Universal's famous 1931 movie, Bela Lugosi warns off his female roommates and sucks the brains out of Renfield. And he has a daughter, and later a son, played by Lon Chaney's son.

Baron Frankenstein wasn't gay. He has a fiancée he avoids, who later becomes his bride, whom he leaves in their wedding bed while he wanders off into the night with Dr. Pretorius, who most definitely *was* gay, *really, really* gay. And Baron Frankenstein had a whole litter of descendants.

Larry Talbot wasn't gay. In fact, in *The Wolfman*, he's something of a wolf before he ever acquires his curse. He even peeps on Evelyn Ankers in her bedroom using an enormous telescope intended for studying the stars.

The monsters weren't gay, except of course they were.

The monsters weren't *intended* to be gay, except possibly when director James Whale was behind the lens, but they read as gay to me. For me and my fellow queer youth growing up in the gay-intolerant era of the mid-twentieth century, these monsters spoke to our lives.

That they flourished in marvelous gothic fantasy films, some brilliant, most ridiculous, all imagination-stirring, only made them more special.

Hollywood's message may have seemed clear: *You're gay; you're a monster. The villagers must hunt you down and destroy you.* However, there was a more subversive underside to them. Almost without exception the monsters are presented sympathetically: Frankenstein's Monster was a lonely innocent, persecuted for existing, and good with children (some of the time). And there was his *enormous schvancestucker.* The Wolfman was a heroic fellow who acquired a cursed life when he came to the aid of a damsel in distress. Even soulless Dracula is often presented as a lonely, isolated figure seeking love, burdened by a curse acquired in defense of his country. The villagers are usually frightened, ignorant yahoos, with a hair-trigger lynch-mob response to almost any stimulus.

These movies said to me, *It is intolerant society that is wrong. Hang in there. Fight the good fight. If you get enough sequels, eventually everyone will love you. Once Abbott and Costello show up, you're home free.*

There is hope.

This book is about those classic cinematic works I loved so much, and love still. If you ever felt like you turned into a monster at the full moon and prowled the streets to find fresh meat to feed your unspeakable hunger, if you ever felt a Forbidden Thirst, if you ever watched Frankenstein's Monster hounded by ignorant, torch-bearing peasants and thought, you and me both, Frankie, or if you ever watched Vincent Price wander the cobwebbed corridors of a lonely mansion late at night and thought, I *want* that dressing gown!, this may be the right book for you.

So come on in. Stay close to the candles; the stairway can be treacherous. And whatever you do, *don't open that door before sunrise!* Let's hope we don't have to delve into Matters Man Was Meant to Leave Alone.

Drat! We do.

The Q Guide

to Classic

Monster Movies

CHAPTER ONE

The Dawn of Dread

QUOTE

"Once upon a
midnight dreary,
While I pondered,
weak and weary,
Over many a quaint
and curious
Volume of forgotten lore . . ."

IT BEGAN IN THE CAVES, IN THE DARK.

What we call cavemen, huddling together in the dark, hearing the sounds in the blackness: rustling, growling, sometimes a scream. And as if what was actually there wasn't bad enough, the nascent imagination of Man populated that darkness with ever-more-horrible monsters of the mind.

As Man acquired more knowledge, he learned about death, and learned what no other living creature on earth knows: that his own death is inevitable. No one liked this fact. One of the many ways Man dealt with it was to invent religion, creating imaginary gods, and later, one imaginary God, who could show favor to His faithful, and assure them that they would live on after death—elaborate systems of belief still in power even today, all for the purpose of denying the inevitable reality of death.

But as the shamans began calling themselves priests, another type of primitive man emerged: the Storyteller. And storytellers dealt with the fear by creating stories, and often these were scary stories of monsters, of dark communions, of an alternative afterlife: Undeath. The listener could shiver in a safe, delicious fear while forgetting the very real, sudden deaths that lurked everywhere, substituting a fake fear for the real thing. At the end of the story, whether it ended with all happy and safe, or with all in ruin and horror, the listener felt better, even relieved. He had faced his fears and conquered them, albeit briefly, only for tonight.

Stories became myths, folklore, legends, and tall tales. Man invented Fiction and Theater, and some writers found themselves fond of getting laughs, others of provoking tears, some of illuminating the heart, and still others of creating the shiver. For the audience has never tired of the shiver, the scream, the adrenaline rush, and the relief when it's all over. Perhaps no other audience response except laughter is so universally popular. Put them together and you always have a winner. As the late Pauline Kael wrote, "Scary-and-funny must be *the* greatest combination for popular entertainment."

The movies were the great popular-entertainment medium for the twentieth century. In the nineteenth century, it was prose fiction. The great monster movies all drew inspiration from literary works of the nineteenth century, in particular, from the writings of four authors: Englishwoman Mary Shelley, Scotsman Robert Louis Stevenson, American Edgar Allan Poe, and Irishman Bram Stoker.

Mary Wollstonecraft Godwin Shelley (1797–1851)

In this year I am writing, Mary Shelley would be 210. Mary, or Little Mary Gloomshine, did not have too happy a life, but clearly she was born to write. Her father, William Godwin, philosopher and atheist, was the author of *An Inquiry Regarding Political Justice,* while her mother, Mary Wollstonecraft, pioneering feminist, was the authoress *of A Vindication of the Rights of Women*. Mary's mother died shortly after giving birth to her, and Mary was raised by a cruel stepmother and an emotionally distant father.

It was their shared atheism that drew Percy Bysshe Shelley to Mary's father, and thus on to her. Over the years of their brief relationship, they had four children, only one of whom survived more than five years. Shelley himself drowned only six years into their marriage. Mary actually kept Shelley's heart as a romantic souvenir, proving she hadn't written *Frankenstein* by accident.

Her most famous work, *Frankenstein, or the Modern Prometheus,* is perhaps the greatest novel ever written by a teenager. The oft-repeated story is that during "The Haunted Summer" of 1816, when Shelley, Mary, Mary's step-sister Claire Clairmont, Claire's lover Lord Byron, and Byron's physician Dr. John Polidori were all staying together on the shores of Lake Geneva, Lord Byron proposed a ghost story-writing competition. Although neither Byron nor Shelley, the literary stars, actually turned out anything of note from this contest, Polidori wrote a novel titled *The Vampire*, more about which shortly.

Mary was stuck for a story idea until, after listening to a conversation on galvanism by the men, she had a nightmare in which she saw an artificially created monster rise up to threaten the medical student who had built it. Fired with enthusiasm, she turned out a short story that Shelley encouraged her to develop into a novel.

Frankenstein is essentially science fiction, before Jules Verne or H.G. Wells, and it isn't Mary's only foray into the genre. There's also her 1826 novel *The Last Man*, relating the end of mankind, wiped off the earth by a plague in the twenty-first century. Try not to panic.

Science never really crossed Mary Shelley's active mind. Her twenty-first century in *The Last Man* is technologically advanced beyond 1826 by about ten minutes. Did you know we still get around on horses? She does see the America Civil War coming, but gets the outcome wrong when she introduces the ambassador from "The Northern States of America." And though she posits the end of human life by 2100, she doesn't ascribe the blame to Karl Rove or Paris Hilton. *Frankenstein, or The Modern Prometheus* is also science lite.

Frankenstein is a dark, bleak, depressing book. It's a

near-classical tragedy that makes *King Lear* look like *Mary Poppins,* but it is also haunting and gripping and, once read, not easily forgotten. Though Mary wrote several more books, it was her only best-seller, and has remained in print for close to 200 years now.

Edgar Allan Poe (1809–1849)

Born twelve years after Mary Shelley, in Boston, Edgar Allan Poe had an even more depressing life than she. He was orphaned at age three. His first wife was his cousin, whom he married when she was thirteen. After her slow, lingering, agonizing death from tuberculosis, a disease that had also claimed Edgar's brother, Edgar's already-heavy drinking got considerably worse. He re-married in 1847, but two years later he was found lying unconscious in a street in Baltimore, and died in a hospital there a few days later.

But during those miserable forty years, Poe turned out a plethora of the finest short horror and mystery tales ever written, as well as much memorable poetry. Is anyone not familiar with the refrain "Quoth the raven, 'Nevermore'"? A prose master whose command of mood can make memorable even tales almost devoid of plot, his influence and popularity remain undimmed more than a century and a half after his sad demise. He is credited with creating the genre of detective fiction, he dabbled in science fiction, and he was also a respected literary critic and essayist. And when I first read his *The Black Cat* when I was ten, it scared the crap out of me.

Robert Louis Stevenson (1850–1894)

Born in Edinburgh, Scotland, the year before Mary Shelley died, Robert Louis Stevenson suffered from tuberculosis almost from birth. At the University of Edinburgh, Stevenson first studied engineering, then law, and passed his bar exam. But once he became a lawyer, he never practiced, instead turning to writing travel sketches and essays. He met his wife, Fanny Osbourne, in France, and they moved first to California, then back to Scotland, and finally to Samoa, where he finished out his forty-four years.

He was a tremendously successful popular novelist, specializing in adventure novels, such as *Kidnapped, The Master of Ballantrae, The Black Arrow,* and the eternally beloved pirate story *Treasure Island.* But Stevenson comes to our attention because of a nightmare he had in 1883, which inspired him to write his novel *The Strange Case of Dr. Jekyll and Mr. Hyde* in just *three days,* which is about how long it took me just to write this chapter. Then he was so horrified by his thrilling story that he burned the manuscript. Then he sat down and wrote it *again,* once more in a mere three days. This time he let it go on to publication, giving us the quintessential novel of the Beast Within.

Perhaps the most breezy, modern read of the Great Monster Triumvirate, new readers coming to it for the first time are often surprised to learn that it is presented as a mystery, with the primary plot twist—*Spoiler*

Alert!—that Jekyll and Hyde are the same man, revealed only in the penultimate chapter, rather than taking the reader along with Jekyll from the start, as all subsequent film versions have done.

Essentially a science-fiction werewolf story, it presents the reader with more interesting moral conundrums than just a simple lycanthropic curse, as Henry Jekyll, the "good" persona, pursues his evil half's lowlife for recreation. It's a swift, fun read, and when I first read it, in fifth grade, it haunted me for weeks.

And between its crowd-pleasing plotline and its natural-acting tour-de-force lead role, it has probably inspired more movies than any other novel.

Bram Stoker (1847–1912)

Born three years before Stevenson, Abraham Stoker was the only one of our quartet to have lived into the twentieth century. Born in Dublin, he was, like Stevenson, a sickly boy. But while Stevenson grew into a sickly man, eventually taking up residence in the South Seas for his health, Stoker not only recovered from his early youthful frailty, but became a robust, active man, and a star athlete at Dublin's Trinity College.

Thrust by his father into a civil-service career, Stoker nonetheless pursued his dream of writing, turning out stories of varying lengths, essays, and even working unpaid as a theater critic for Dublin's *Evening Mail*.

But in 1878, Stoker left the civil service, and instead became the manager of London's Lyceum Theatre, personal preserve of Sir Henry Irving, the greatest star of the English stage at that time. That same year Stoker married Florence Balcombe, a strong-willed woman who had earlier wisely refused a marital proposal from Oscar Wilde. They had one son, Noel.

Sometime in the 1890s, after a particularly large and rich meal, Stoker had a nightmare in which he saw a vampire king rise from his grave to batten on the living, and like Mary Shelley and R.L. Stevenson before him, he was inspired by his evil dream to write an enduring novel of an iconic monster. Influenced by John Polidori's novel *The Vampire*, the first story known to have portrayed a vampire as nobleman, Lord Ruthven, rather than the usual lowly human-peasant vermin as they had previously been portrayed, Stoker did some research, and discovered the then-obscure historical figure Vlad Tepes, King of Romania off and on back in the fifteenth century, a man of surpassing cruelty and viciousness, almost legendary for the tortures and murders he committed, yet still considered a hero in Romania for his defense of Christianity against the invading Muslim forces of Turkey.

Stoker took one of Vlad's many names, Dracula, which meant "Little Dragon" or "Little Devil," but which actually indicated only that he was the son of Draco, his almost-as-nasty father, and Stoker christened his vampire lord Count Dracula. Deciding that perhaps Vlad Dracula had sold his soul to the devil for military victories against the Turks, Stoker had his cruel feudal lord surviving into the nineteenth century by feeding on the blood of the living, and then moving to then-modern London, to spread this archaic plague among the panting virgins of Victorian society.

As literature, *Dracula* is the low end of our scale

here. Even the turgid *Frankenstein* is better written and more literarily respectable. But *Dracula*'s pulp-fiction thrills made it an immediate best-seller on its publication in 1897, exactly a century after the birth of Mary Shelley, and it has never gone out of print. As pulp fiction goes, it's very good. Nothing Stoker wrote before or after had anything like its power. Yet even with his new status as a best-selling novelist, he continued to work for Sir Henry Irving while still writing on the side. He died in 1912, of "locomotor ataxy," a form of insanity commonly associated with syphilis. Florence Stoker remained healthy.

Although a number of Victorian-era writers, Henry James, M.R. James (no relation), and E.F. Benson high among them, turned out memorable ghost stories, it was these four writers, more than anyone else, who set the stage for the movie monsters we would soon come to love.

CHAPTER TWO

The Fear Factories

QUOTE

"I am Dracula. Welcome to my home. Enter freely, and of your own will."

HOLLYWOOD, THEY SAY, IS A STATE OF MIND. Perhaps. But it's also a section of Los Angeles real estate long thought of as the home of the motion-picture industry. Actually, only a few of the major studios are in Hollywood: Paramount, RKO, and Columbia. MGM, Hal Roach, and Selznick International were west, in Culver City. 20th Century Fox is on the western edge of Beverly Hills (the stars could walk to work, like that would ever happen). Warner Bros. and Disney are over the hill in Burbank (Disney began in Silverlake, off the easternmost end of Hollywood), and Universal remains just north of Hollywood, over and on the hill, in Studio City.

Though each studio made forays into almost every genre, each had specialties for which it became known. MGM and 20th had their musicals, family dramas, and women's pictures. Warner Bros. had tough melodramas and gangster epics. Disney had animation and family entertainment. Roach was slapstick comedy heaven, while Paramount in 1934 had Mae West, W.C. Fields and the Marx Brothers all turning out the greatest comedies of all time just yards from each other and, a decade later, Preston Sturgis making the most sophisticated romantic comedies ever.

And from 1934 on, Universal was synonymous with one word: *monsters*.

Carl Laemmle, who founded Universal Studios in 1912, didn't want to make horror movies. He had to be dragged into the genre by his son. Carl was a genre snob, and horror was, and often still is, considered low-class exploitation entertainment.

No studio was associated with horror in the silent era. Most of Lon Chaney's often-frightening movies were made for MGM, although the two most famous, *The Hunchback of Notre Dame* and *The Phantom of the Opera*, were made for Universal. But *Hunchback* was considered a prestigious literary adaptation, while *Phantom* was considered merely a particularly grotesque melodrama. The very term *horror movie* didn't exist until Universal released *Dracula* in 1931.

Carl Laemmle Jr. happened to be in the audience when the stage adaptation of *Dracula* starring Bela Lugosi opened on Broadway in 1927. Little Carl immediately began pressuring daddy to acquire the film rights, and while Big Carl (actually both men were quite short) turned up his nose at the gothic fantasy, he wasn't too proud to covet the huge grosses the hoary melodrama was amassing both in New York and in London's West End.

By 1930, *Dracula* was in active development at Universal, intended as a vehicle for Lon Chaney. But when Chaney died of throat cancer that year, the role eventually went to Lugosi. Opening on Valentine's Day, 1931, the picture was a gigantic hit. *Frankenstein* was rushed into production, and actually was in theaters before the year ended. With *Frankenstein* an even bigger hit (and a *much* better movie) than *Dracula,* Universal had found its niche—much to Big Carl's chagrin—and would release more than 50 monster or horror movies over the next two decades. Although mostly a television production facility and proprietor of theme parks today, its association with monster movies continues with such recent releases as *The Mummy, The Mummy Returns,* and *Van Helsing.*

Other studios noted Universal's monster profits, and made the occasional foray into Monsterland. Although Louis B. Mayer *hated* monster movies even more than Big Carl, he wasn't too snobbish to let MGM turn out Boris Karloff's hilarious *The Mask of Fu Manchu,* Bela Lugosi's absurd *Mark of the Vampire,* Peter Lorre's bizarre *Mad Love,* and Tod Browning's frightening, extremely disturbing, and financially quite unsuccessful *Freaks,* a movie Mayer loathed.

Paramount turned out a superior *Dr. Jekyll and Mr. Hyde* in 1932, and an unsettlingly scary *Island of Lost Souls,* loosely adapted from an H.G. Wells novel (Wells felt it was a vulgarization of his haunting book) in 1933.

Warner Bros. made a string of thrillers, some in two-color Technicolor: *The Mystery of the Wax Museum, Doctor X,* and *The Return of Doctor X.*

The only really serious challenger to Universal's supremacy in the monster-thriller genre prior to the 1950s was RKO, with *The Most Dangerous Game, King Kong, Son of Kong,* and the supremely silly *She,* in the thirties, and a series of nine superb thrillers, *Cat People, Curse of the Cat People, I Walked with a Zombie, The Ghost Ship, The Leopard Man, The Seventh Victim, The Body Snatcher, Isle of the Dead,* and *Bedlam,* all produced by Val Lewton in the forties.

Columbia came late to the game with Karloff's *The Black Room,* and then employed him as almost a whole think-tank of mad scientists in the forties in such thrillers as *The Man They Could Not Hang, The Man With Nine Lives, Before I Hang,* and *The Devil Commands.*

Why were these movies so popular in the thirties and forties? Societal fears always drive monster popularity. As back in the caves, one enjoys a scary story to spend some time replacing real anxieties with safe, imaginary terrors. In the thirties, the depredations of the Depression, combined with the international tensions building towards the explosion that was World War II, fueled the ticket sales of Universal's monsters.

Further, during World War I, medicine had progressed to where many more of the seriously wounded could be saved than ever before, but it had not progressed enough to reconstruct their appearances, which left an unprecedented number of massively disfigured war survivors in society. One encountered the pitiably monstrous-looking in large cities on a daily basis. Again, it was monster movies that helped society process the conflicting emotions this phenomenon raised.

Do I really need to tell you what all the world was anxious about during World War II? The wolf people were on the march in Europe, Asia, and the Pacific. Is it any wonder that the folks at home sought emotional refuge in movies about werewolves and vampires? And these movies, far more often than not, were written and/or directed by refugees from Hitler's horrors.

After the massive global horror of World War II ended, the monster genre receded for a decade, as people tried to tell themselves that evil had been vanquished once and for all. Abbott and Costello, Universal's *other* reliable stars, met all Universal's monsters in turn, while low-budget, forgettable B- and Z-level movies crept out of fly-by-night independents, and Vincent Price moved up from character actor to star status in the Warner Bros. 3-D one-off *House of Wax*. Only one new monster emerged in the decade, when Universal worked its old magic one last time, in the 3-D picture *Creature From the Black Lagoon,* which spawned two fairly good sequels.

But in the wake of Hiroshima, science-fiction replaced gothics, and when Earth wasn't battling alien invasions in *War of the Worlds, The Thing from Another World, Invasion of the Body Snatchers, Earth vs. the Flying Saucers,* and *It Came from Outer Space* (and their low-budget imitations, like *The Man From Planet X* and *It, the Terror from Beyond Space*—although *It* only came from Mars, which is *in* space, not *beyond* it), we were battling giant, radiation-spawned monsters like the giant ants of *Them,* the giant grasshoppers of *The Beginning of the End,* the giant octopus of *It Came from Beneath the Sea* (there were *It*s all over the place), and whole herds of atomically revived dinosaurs, from *The Beast From 20,000 Fathoms* to the bewilderingly beloved *Godzilla, King of the Monsters*.

However, it was not until 1957 that another studio claimed the mantle of Fear Factory. That year, England's Hammer Studios, which had made a pound or two with black-and-white science-fiction movies like *X, the Unknown* and their two *Quatermass* films, decided to try a Technicolor gothic, and made *The Curse of Frankenstein*, which was an enormous international success and made monster icons of Peter Cushing and Christopher Lee. For the next twenty-six years, Hammer was to turn out an amazing string of color gothics, putting a decidedly British gloss on their remakes of Universal's classic monsters, until their output finally puttered out in the early seventies, mired in a now-worn-out formula.

Hammer's success hardly went unnoticed in the United States, where its movies were hugely popular. American International Pictures, a low-budget production company without even studio facilities to call their own, had been making scads of Z-movie thrillers that seemed to cost even less than a ticket to see them, when Roger Corman, a man who could squeeze a production penny until Lincoln screamed, persuaded studio heads James H. Nicholson (no relation to AIP's most successful discovery, Jack Nicholson) and Samuel Z. Arkoff to double his budget and increase his production time (from one week to three), in order to make a color Cinemascope gothic adaptation of Poe's *Fall of the House of Usher* starring Vincent Price. Its enormous success (it was one of the three highest-grossing movies of 1960, along with *Psycho* and *Spartacus*) led AIP, as Universal and Hammer had been led before it, into producing a long string of color horror movies, most starring Price, while aging monster icons Karloff, Peter Lorre, Lon Chaney Jr., and Basil Rathbone finished out their careers picking up paychecks for sharing that widescreen frame with Price.

Since the heydays of Hammer and AIP, no other studio has claimed that mantle again, nor has any other actor taken the iconic mantles last worn by Price and Cushing, and still belonging to the amazing Christopher Lee. Sorry, Robert Englund, playing Freddy Krueger in a series of movies doesn't make you the new Boris Karloff.

But the day may still come when another studio will find a new gothic formula for the twenty-first century, and a worthy successor to Chaney, Lugosi, Karloff, Price, Cushing, and Lee may emerge. Meanwhile, let's take a Q look at some of the best of the classics.

"No one can deny the indefinable charm."

On October 20, 1882, Bela Ferenc Dezso Blasko was born in Lugoj (pronounced *Lugosh*), Hungary. On February 14, 1931, having dropped most of his American-movie-publicity-unfriendly names and replacing them with a mild corruption of the name of his hometown, "Bela Lugosi" became a movie star.

Bela was the youngest of four children. The strong-willed son of a strong-willed father, Bela left home at the age of twelve. Unable to get an acting career rolling at twelve, Bela became one of the many twelve-year-old minor miners no sensible economy is without. Eight years after leaving home, Bela made his stage debut.

For the next two decades, Bela played hundreds of different roles onstage, including his favorite one to flaunt when he became an America star, Jesus Christ. The existing photographs of Bela as Jesus show us what looks like Dracula in a hippie phase, and showing enough manflesh to raise less-than-holy thoughts in his female and gay-male public. He appeared in various roles in a lot of Shakespeare's plays, albeit translated into Hungarian, which I'm sure improves them greatly.

We are told that Lugosi was a much-admired actor in Hungary, though we were mostly told this by Bela. He did become a member of Hungary's National Theater, though not in leads. He enlisted in the Hungarian army during World War I. Bela was fond of telling gullible publicists in Hollywood that he had been a hangman in the army, though no proof of his grisly occupation survives, if ever it existed.

After the war, Bela aligned himself with a revolutionary movement. When the revolution failed, he was declared a traitor and fled to Vienna, a political refugee. He emigrated to America in 1921. By the time he was cast as Count Dracula on Broadway in 1927, he had still not learned English, and was memorizing his dialogue phonetically, but even after he had finally learned the language, his trademark overplaying never lessened.

Bela still has many fans and rabid devotees, people who believe he was a great actor. Even at his worst, he was enjoyable, and no one can deny the indefinable charm that existed between him and the camera he seldom held back for.

His Count Dracula was so on-the-nose vocally, and one of his most underplayed roles, that it comes across fairly well, both in *Dracula* and, even better, in *Abbott & Costello Meet Frankenstein*. But as early as his first post-*Dracula* starring role, Dr. Mirakle in *Murders in the Rue Morgue,* he is in the full flower of the wild overacting that sadly became his real trademark. It lost him his Universal contract. Barely a year after *Dracula,* he was appearing in serials and low-budget programmers like *White Zombie.*

Lugosi got the occasional non-horror role, such as

his small parts as Russians in W.C. Fields's *International House* and Garbo's *Ninotchka*. No one left the theater discussing his performance, but perhaps that was a good thing.

They did leave the theater discussing his performance in *Son of Frankenstein*, as the broken-necked shepherd/grave-robber, Ygor. It may be his finest performance in a movie. He's unrecognizable both visually and audibly. His performance is big and broad without being *too* big and broad, and his relationship with the Monster is genuinely touching.

But by the forties, the use of him in *The Wolf Man* is more typical, slipped into a five-minute role too small for him to damage the movie, strictly to put his name in the credits. His *Abbott & Costello* romp in 1948 was his last major-studio motion picture. The degradations of *Old Mother Riley Meets the Vampire, Bela Lugosi Meets a Brooklyn Gorilla,* and the trash of Ed Wood lay not far ahead.

Bela arrived at Universal for *Dracula* with three short marriages already behind him, their quick terminations generally ascribed to his jealousy. The love of his life was clearly his fourth wife, Lillian, the mother of his only child, Bela Jr. But even Lillian eventually couldn't take his dark moods as his career sank and his tragic morphine addiction rose, so she divorced Bela and later married Brian Donlevy.

Bela, like many another star from Peter Lorre to Judy Garland, became hooked on painkillers prescribed by studio Dr. Feelgoods. It is to his everlasting credit that he not only triumphed over his addiction, but became the first Hollywood star ever to go public with his rehab.

Sadly, the rigors of detoxing took their toll on the elderly, frail actor, and he lived only a few months longer. His pathetic last marriage was to a fan named Hope, but she was really His Last Hope. She wanted Dracula, and what she got was a very old, weak, washed-up, foul-tempered, former star, and rather than being touched by his plight and giving him the gift of a final, sustaining love, she took out her disappointment and disillusionment on him, treating him harshly and depriving him of the respect he deserved.

His sad final months came to a quiet end when his heart simply stopped beating while he slept on August 16, 1956, in his home in Hollywood. He was, supposedly according to his wishes, buried in one of his Dracula capes.

Bela would be surprised and pleased to learn not only that he is still remembered, but that he still has thousands of fans. He has indeed become undead.

CHAPTER THREE

The Golden Age

The Films of the 1930s

QUOTE

"Mr. Carl Laemmle feels it would be a little unkind to present this picture without just a word of friendly warning."

THE 1930S WERE THE GOLDEN AGE of the monster movie. In 1930, there was basically no such thing as a monster-movie genre. But when *Dracula* was a surprise, studio-saving-sized hit, and *Frankenstein* was even bigger, the floodgates were unleashed, and for five years, monsters poured out of Universal at a steady rate, with other studios making the occasional contribution.

In 1936, the Laemmle's lost possession of Universal. Concurrent with the Laemmles losing Universal, the British blue-noses clamped down on horror movies. With the lucrative English market dead to scary movies, Hollywood gave them up. Universal began making an entirely new kind of horror movie, ones starring Deanna Durbin. Karloff found other work easily, but Bela Lugosi, not sweepingly admired by an industry that had seen his acting, faced fifteen months of unemployment, and lost his house.

Then, in 1938, a triple feature of *Dracula, Frankenstein,* and *Son of Kong* unexpectedly hit a box-office jackpot. The new Universal brass—or, rather, the *new* new Universal brass, as the first Laemmle replacements were already gone, drowned in a sea of red ink—saw what was happening, and quickly rushed a new Frankenstein movie into production. So in 1939, the genre, like Dracula and Frankenstein's Monster themselves, rose from its grave. Although the new wave of monster movies that began with *Son of Frankenstein* in 1939 belong properly to the Silver Age of the 1940s, *Son of Frankenstein* was such a spectacular one-off that I prefer to see it as the last of the great Golden-Age monsters.

So here's the Top-Ten Monster Movies of the 1930s, in order of release, not quality, followed by a briefer glance at some honorable mentions.

The Top-Ten Golden Age Monster Movies

1. Dracula *(Universal, 1931)*

"To die, to be really dead, that must be glorious."

Of all the American films ever to have achieved the status of Beloved Classic Movie, *Dracula* is without doubt the worst, a dull, stagy, static bore. Once the action catches up to the play, abandon hope, all ye who remain awake.

The Story: Real-estate agent R. (Ralph?) Renfield, ignoring the advice of primitive peasants, travels to the castle of elderly (about 400 years old) Count Dracula in the Carpathian Mountains of Transylvania, to handle the details of Dracula's move to London, only to get seduced and sucked by the ancient predator. Dracula and the now-insane Renfield travel to England, where Renfield is committed to an asylum, while Dracula sucks his way through the female cast, until crusty Professor Van Helsing pounds a phallic stake through his heart, and peace is re-established, at least until the sequel.

Dracula gives us our first-ever glimpse of Universal's Evil Neverland, its fairy-tale anti-Oz. Castle Dracula looks wonderful. I want to move in today. Inside, it is a gothic wet dream of a spooky ruin. This vast, fabulous set, with its giant staircase, its enormous spiderweb, and a tree growing in through an immense shattered window, gets slightly less than three minutes of screen time. We will eventually stare at Dr. Seward's boring drawing room for what seems like hours, but we get just three minutes in this great set.

The first fifteen minutes, though slowly paced, look great, and have a really wonderful, spooky atmosphere. But after fifteen minutes, the movie grinds to a dead halt.

Garrett Fort's screenplay for *Dracula* is often faulted for relying too much on the stage play, but the lack of any basic film-making technique is what really kills it. In *Dracula,* the camera just sits there a great deal of the

SHE LIVES!

In the opening scene of *Dracula*, a coach is traveling to Castle Dracula. Inside the coach, Renfield is being bored by a bespectacled lass with a piercing nasal voice reading a travel book of Transylvanian exposition aloud, before a bump in the road sends her face into a man's lap, much to the sneering contempt of her bull-dyke companion.

The lass in question is Carla Laemmle. No, not one of the Carls in drag, but rather a niece of Big Carl enjoying a little nepotistic casting. ("No, no," says Little Carl from his grave, "She was the *best possible choice* for the role.") Today (the day I am writing—I hope it is time, watching the cast talk in endless medium shots, without a close-up or change of angle to wake us up.

Bela Lugosi's performance is static and slow to the point of being dreary, though there's no mistaking his magnetism, either, and the halting, unfamiliar delivery is very right for a 400-year-old feudal lord who has learned English from books. If he lacks the menace others have brought to Dracula, he still has a weird otherworldliness that befits the character. And he stamped it so indelibly that even today, when we have had *much* better Draculas from *much* better actors, many still consider him the gold standard. I can't say he is good in *Dracula*, but he isn't yet terrible. And whatever he was, he was not what was worst about *Dracula*.

still true when you read this), Miss Laemmle is the last living survivor of *Dracula*. When I met her a few months ago, I suggested to her that it was mighty suspicious that the last survivor of the movie was the niece of the studio head. "Coincidence," I asked her, "Or—*murder?*" She went with coincidence, and I didn't challenge her, as I didn't want to be the next to die.

Miss Laemmle made her screen debut at sixteen in the Lon Chaney classic *The Phantom of the Opera*. As the lead ballerina at the opera, she is in the opening sequence of that great silent monster movie as well. She was there at the start of Universal's monster *oeuvre*. Perhaps someone really did find immortality.

The film is afraid to be shocking. The climax of *Dracula* is one of the big letdowns of all time. Renfield, played with a manic gusto that brings the movie what little energy it has, drops in at Carfax Abbey, Dracula's London digs, for no reason. Van Helsing, played boringly with an astonishing degree of stolid, pompous blather by Edward Van Sloan, also a veteran of the Broadway production, and "romantic" lead Jonathon Harker, played effeminately by gay actor David Manners, also wander by for no reason. Dracula and Mina, played as a listless dishrag without enough blood to attract even a vampire by Helen Chandler, arrive via a different route. This momentary, arbitrary, coincidental convergence takes the place of Bram Stoker's climactic

THE OTHER *DRACULA*

Made at the same time as *Dracula* was *Drácula*, Universal's Spanish-language version, shot on the same sets, utilizing the same script, but with a director, George Melford, who wanted to show the world, or at least the Carls, that he was a *director*. Both films are available on the same DVD, and they make a fascinating comparison. The Spanish *Drácula* is *vastly* better, this despite being weighed down with an actor playing *Conde Drácula*, Carlos Villarías, who made Bela Lugosi look like a master of subtlety and nuance.

trans-European chase by boat, train, and horseback. Five people wander aimlessly into the same yard. Much better than a big chase. Well, cheaper anyway.

Van Helsing hammers a wooden slat through Dracula *off-screen*. We hear a groan. That's it. I'm *so* scared. Anyway, it's over. Some chimes chime, probably to wake up the audience to leave.

Opening on Valentine's Day, as befits this tender tale of a gay corpse raping the living, *Dracula* was a gigantic hit, one of the biggest grossing movies of 1931. The Carls got the message. *Frankenstein* was greenlit, *Dracula* would spawn five sequels, and the horror boom of the 1930s was off and flapping. It had nowhere to go but up.

It wasn't the script; it was the same script Tod Browning was shooting. The pacing can't be credited with the improvement; the Spanish *Drácula* is half an hour *longer* than the English one. Nor, as implied above, is it the acting. It's the camera, which moves about, finding us stuff to look at. It's the more-interesting lighting. It's the eerier effects. In the last analysis, it's a director who cared about what he was doing. And Melford didn't even speak Spanish.

Lupita Tovar, who played the female lead, married the producer, and still lives on today, testifies that the cast and crew looked at Browning's rushes and decided to prove that they could do better. They did.

2. Frankenstein *(Universal, 1931)*

"In the name of God, now I know what it feels like to be God!"

The Story: Brilliant but high-strung medical student Henry Frankenstein and his posture-challenged assistant Fritz are conducting an experiment in the artificial creation of human life. They rob graves, and steal a criminal brain from the local university, stitching together a patchwork corpse, which they then imbue with life. The innocent creature, mistreated by the sadistic Fritz and abandoned by its creator, escapes from the lab, and acts out by going on a killing spree. When it accidentally drowns a little girl, Henry is forced to postpone his wedding and lead a torch-bearing mob in pursuit of the Monster. Henry and his creature confront each other in an old mill. The Monster tosses Henry off a balcony, and then is burned to death in the mill by the mob. Henry survives his fall and marries his neglected fiancée.

The role of the Frankenstein Monster was haughtily refused by Bela Lugosi. Noted author Gregory William Mank quotes Lugosi as saying: "I will not be a grunting, babbling idiot for anybody! I need a part where I can *act!*"

The direction was handed to the openly gay English genius James Whale. Whale immediately proved his genius by almost literally plucking Boris Karloff from the crowd to replace Lugosi in the role of the Monster, and, as it turned out to Lugosi's everlasting ire, also as Universal's number-one bogeyman. Karloff instantly saw that the Monster *was* a part where he could *act*, and act it he did, right into the hearts and dark bedroom corners of America, and the resulting movie set the Fránkenstein myth in concrete for all time.

Dwight Frye and Edward Van Sloan were drafted from the *Dracula* cast for similar roles, while David Manners was replaced in the romantic lead by the even duller John Boles. Bette Davis was briefly considered for Elizabeth, but Carl Laemmle thought she was ugly, and the part went to Mae Clark, who was pretty and talented, but no Bette Davis. Clark's greatest fame would come that same year, when James Cagney used her face as a fruit juicer in *The Public Enemy*.

Shot only ten months after *Dracula*, *Frankenstein* is a vastly better movie. Brilliantly directed by Whale, gorgeously designed by Whale, Jack Pierce, Charles

D. Hall, and Herman Rosse, magnificently photographed by Arthur Edeson, who would go on to shoot *The Maltese Falcon* and *Casablanca,* well-acted by all, except arguably Edward Van Sloan and Mae Clark, and featuring Boris Karloff giving one of the greatest acting performances in the history of American cinema, *Frankenstein* holds up as a still-great movie.

Karloff's Monster is a pathetic innocent with a nasty temper. Nightmarishly scary-looking? You bet. But also lovable from his first entrance almost halfway through the film. And damn if he isn't even kind of sexy, in a primitive-brute sort of way.

Frankenstein was an even bigger hit than *Dracula,* which makes sense, as it is so very much better. It may not frighten anyone anymore, but I suspect today's ten-year-olds may still find themselves haunted by it as strongly as I was the first time I saw it, back in 1962.

3. Freaks *(MGM, 1932)*

"Offend one, and you offend them all."

Lon Chaney, Myrna Loy, Victor McLaglen, and Jean Harlow in *Freaks*! Remember that cast? No? Not surprising. Between MGM's acquisition of the short story *Spurs,* and *Freaks* actually facing the cameras, Lon Chaney died, Myrna Loy *hated* the script and begged Irving Thalberg to release her from the picture, and Harlow and McLaglen were recast at the last minute. *Freaks* ended up starring Wallace Ford, Olga Baclanova, Leila Hyams, and Henry Victor. And it really mattered little, because the handful of people who saw *Freaks* between its release in early 1932 and when the studio withdrew it and locked it away a few months later remembered only the rest of the cast, the large group of genuine circus-sideshow freaks.

The Story: Lustful little person Hans, though engaged to his equally small girlfriend Frieda, only has eyes for the tall, cruel queen of the trapeze, Cleopatra. Animal trainer Venus leaves brutal strongman Hercules for the sympathetic clown Phroso. Hercules begins an affair with Cleopatra, and aids her in milking expensive gifts out of Hans. When one of the gifts is a platinum bracelet worth thousands, they begin to wonder where Hans is getting so much money. Frieda accidentally lets slip to Cleopatra that Hans has inherited an enormous fortune.

Cleopatra marries Hans, and begins poisoning him almost at once. At the wedding banquet, the freaks welcome Olga into their ranks, chanting "One of us. One of us." Repulsed, Olga, who is extremely drunk, lashes out at them, calling them slimy freaks, and drenching a dwarf with champagne.

The freaks begin spying on Olga, and quickly discover her affair with Hercules and that she is poisoning Hans. Venus confronts Hercules and warns him to leave Hans alone.

As the circus caravan travels through a thunderstorm, Hans confronts Olga, demanding the poison. At the same time, Hercules tries to kill Venus, but she is defended by Phroso. The caravan runs into a ditch, and the freaks swarm after Olga and Hercules through the mud and the lightening. Hercules is knifed, and Olga is cornered beside a tree. Some years later, we find Olga being exhibited in a freak show as a chicken woman, covered in feathers, deprived of legs, and able only to squawk. In an epilogue, Hans and Frieda are reunited in Hans's lavish home by Venus and Phroso. Frieda reminds him that he only demanded the poison from Olga; it was the other freaks who mutilated her.

Director Tod Browning had spent years working in circuses and sideshows, and many of his silent movies, like the brilliant Lon Chaney picture *The Unknown,* are set in circuses, and were remarkable for their reliably accurate portrayal of circus life. *Freaks* is a backstage-at-the-circus story where we barely glimpse the performances. The focus is strictly on the performers's lives away from the center ring. For all it's melodramatic horror, it is vastly more authentic than Cecil B. DeMille's multimillion-dollar epic piece of Oscar-winning claptrap, *The Greatest Show on Earth.*

Freaks is probably the most disturbing of all 1930s movies. Audiences at the time *hated* it. It was often met with outright loathing, and the studio eventually withdrew it from circulation, and it went almost unseen until the 1960s. It is a great and powerful film, but I had to force myself to watch it again, for the first time in thirty-seven years, to write this overview, as it is not a pleasant sixty-two minutes.

The picture wears its liberal, tolerant credentials up front. In an early scene, an outraged groundskeeper beseeches his landlord to throw out the monstrosities trespassing on his lands. But when the landlord finds only innocent, childlike circus freaks having a picnic and a romp in the sun, away from the circus for a day, he invites them to stay as long as they like, and even this old cynic got moist-eyed. The film presents itself as representing the freaks' point of view, championing them over the cruel normal humans.

But the film undeniably exploits the freaks for their inherent creepiness. The sweet, mentally disabled "pinheads" are a case in point. In the picnic scene and a few others, we experience their charming, childlike, sweet innocence, the unfeigned reality of these three people. But when, in the climax, we see one of the microcephalics crawling through the mud brandishing a large knife, and are expected to be frightened by her, the extreme bad taste of handing a knife to a mentally disabled girl, and then shooting her for maximum horror pulled me completely out of the scene, repelled by the bad taste of using this innocent woman-child this way. (The most charming of the microcephalics, Schlitze, is treated as a girl, wears a dress, and is billed in the closing credits as being played "by herself." "She" is a male.)

One of the most memorable shots in the climax shows Prince Randian, the "Living Torso," a man born with no arms or legs, wriggling through the mud with a knife clenched in his teeth. As a nightmare image, it's unforgettable. As a logical menace, it's meaningless. What's he going to do? Spit the knife at Olga? Wriggle on her?

And there's almost no end to the creepy, exploitative, sexual side of things, inescapable because the film keeps insisting on it. The plot revolves around a reverse–King Kong romance. Instead of a male in love with a woman smaller than his genitalia, we have a woman romancing a man who comes up to her knees.

A subplot revolves around the marriage of one of a

pair of female Siamese twins (the world-famous Hilton Sisters, not to be confused with our current freak Hilton Sisters) and the engagement of the other, and leers at the idea of their bedroom arrangements. And the husband of the one Siamese twin plays a woman in the sideshow. One character is Josephine Joseph, a "half-man, half-woman." Though supposedly a genuine hermaphrodite, I doubt real hermaphrodites are sexually divided up the middle, vertically. In any event, the sniggering jokes about him/her are frequent. The Bearded Lady gives birth to a baby, as her husband, the "Living Skeleton," boasts that he's trying his best for more kids, just to rub our noses in the image of this deformed man and his hairy woman, procreating.

And even the normal humans are subjected to amazing pre-production-code sexual leering and mangling. Double entendres fill the dialogue. In one scene, Venus appears to chat with Phroso while he bathes nude in front of her, only to have him emerge, wearing pants, from *under* the tub, which turns out to be a clown prop for a bath gag he is working out. When Venus first shows a romantic interest in him, he says, "You should have seen me before my operation." And in the original ending, Hercules was castrated, and was to be last seen singing soprano in the circus.

As if the film's sexual leering isn't bad enough, Hans and Frieda, the little-people lovers, are played by a real-life brother and sister, and their enormous resemblance to each other makes the romantic scenes between them even more flesh-creeping. (Hans and Frieda both played Munchkins in *The Wizard of Oz*. Hans is the Lollipop Guild Munchkin on the right end.) On the DVD, we are told that Prince Randian was taken care of by his son. How that conception took place is an image I can not scrub from my brain.

Most of the freaks who appeared in the picture remembered it with varying degrees of regret. Most, in interviews, expressed distaste for the picture, and some went so far as to refuse ever to discuss it at all.

Yet it is an undeniably powerful film. If you see it, you won't forget it, but you may wish you could.

4. The Mummy *(1932)*

"I loved you once, but now you belong with the dead."

In the wake of *Frankenstein*'s enormous success, Boris Karloff was a huge star, and Universal was scrambling to find vehicles for him. The brouhaha about the supposed curse of King Tut's tomb inspired Carl Laemmle Jr. to retool a treatment for a film on the famous charlatan-magician Cagliostro into an Egyptian-themed Karloff-film.

The Story: A pair of British archeologists unearth the mummy of an ancient priest, 3,700-year-old Imhotep, as well as the Scroll of Thoth, which every school-kid knows was used by Isis to raise Osiris from the dead. When one of the scientists reads the scroll aloud, Imhotep wakes up, steals the scroll, and wanders off into the night, to the never-ending amusement of the scientist, who literally dies laughing.

Eleven years later, Imhotep, now calling himself Ardath Bey, leads another team of British archeologists to the unplundered tomb of the Princess Anck-es-en-Amon, so they can plunder it. Anck-es-en-Amon was

Imhotep's forbidden girlfriend back in Ancient Egypt, and Ardath intends to restore her to life as he was restored. But her soul has been reincarnated as Helen Grosvenor. Ardath Bey tries to kill Helen, so she can be resurrected as a living mummy like himself, telling her she must "face moments of horror for an eternity of love," neatly describing many a wedding night. The Princess's repentant prayers to Isis prompt the goddess to intervene, divinely killing Imhotep and reducing his body to dust. The Scroll of Thoth burns.

Karl Freund, the 360-pound genius cinematographer, who had shot *The Golem, Metropolis, All Quiet on the Western Front,* and *Dracula,* was given the assignment of making his directorial debut with *The Mummy.* Freund's camera keeps *The Mummy* from ever lapsing into boredom.

The day they shot the scene where Imhotep awakens from the dead was a miserable day for Boris. He had spent eight hours having Jack Pierce laboriously apply the make-up and the bandages he wears. Every account of this film emphasizes this ordeal, as though Karloff spent *every* day of the shoot enduring eight hours in make-up before filming could begin. Actually, he wore this extreme make-up, which looks great though it does not resemble an actual mummy at all, on only a single shooting day. The rest of the time he wore the far less arduous and time-consuming Ardath Bey make-up.

Beautifully directed and shot by Freund, well-acted by Zita Johann and Karloff, devoid of any humor or comic relief, and using lighting and mood more than shock and violence to achieve its effects, *The Mummy* rises above its absurdities to remain a potent chiller that reminds us that after age forty, give it up. Unnatural sex is for the young only. Thank you, Karl Freund, and fuck you.

Karloff's Ardath Bey looks great for a man his age: tall, whip-thin, befezzed like the world's most sinister Shriner, jet-black eyebrows, skin admittedly in serious need of some moisturizer, and speaking perfect English. Karloff keeps all movement to the barest minimum, and avoids all physical contact. His stillness commands the screen. And his resemblance to an erection is hard to miss also.

Helen and Princess Anck-es-en-Amon are played by the exotic Hungarian actress Zita Johann, a flat-chested knockout of a beauty.

The shots of Karloff being wrapped up in his mummy bandages while still alive and struggling are truly horrifying, and can still creep you out today.

Sadly, we are again treated to Edward Van Sloan's ponderous pompousness, and to David Manners's effeminate version of a macho hero. Manners's swishy Frank Whemple is a remarkably dim bulb for a scientist. At one point, Frank says, "Queer story[!], that young Oxford chap going mad. You know what I think it was?"

"No, what?" says fellow archeologist Dr. Pearson.

"I think he went crazy," Frank has razor-sharp deductive powers.

Later in the picture, Frank would sound like a love-happy teenage boy as he says, "Do you think I have a chance?" if he weren't saying it with his father's fresh corpse *literally lying at his feet*. Frank manages, via deft footwork, not to stumble over his dad's cadaver as he dashes over to call Helen and make a date.

Universal never made a sequel to *The Mummy*. The Laemmles realized they had a one-off. Besides, when the Goddess Isis reduces your leading character to dust, even a Hollywood mogul can't bring him back.

5. King Kong *(RKO, 1933)*

"It was beauty killed the beast."

There are monsters, and then, there are *MONSTERS!* King Kong, the Eighth Wonder of the World, was the biggest monster anyone had ever seen. Twenty years later, Japan's *Gojira* was released in America as *Godzilla, King of the Monsters*, but we weren't fooled. Kong was the once and future king. In 1933, no one had ever seen anything like him.

The Story: Fly-by-night adventure-movie producer Carl Denham recruits a Depression-impoverished actress off the street and onto a ship, and sails for a remote, uncharted South Seas island on the basis of a most dubious map, looking for the greatest thing anyone has ever seen. On the voyage, the girl, Ann Darrow, falls in love with the surly-but-handsome first mate, Jack Driscoll. On the island they improbably find a tribe of black natives, instead of the Polynesians one would expect, tending a gigantic, ancient wall. The natives kidnap the blond Darrow, and offer her as a sacrifice to their pagan god, as "The Bride of Kong."

The god turns out to be a thirty-foot gorilla, who makes off with his human prize into the jungle behind the wall. Pursuing her, the movie crew finds living prehistoric dinosaurs, and most of the rescue party is killed. Driscoll frees Ann from the giant ape, but Kong chases them back to the wall. Breaking through the giant doors, Kong rampages through the native village, until Denham lays him out with gas bombs.

Somehow they manage to transport the immense beast back to New York City and into a Broadway theater, where he is exhibited as "The Eighth Wonder of the World." When Kong misinterprets camera flashbulbs for an attack upon Ann, he breaks loose, grabs Ann back, and wreaks havoc and destruction on midtown Manhattan, until a quartet of bi-planes are able to shoot him off the top of the newly completed Empire State Building, as Jack again rescues Ann.

Visual hyperbole was the underlying appeal of *King Kong*, underscored by grand spectacle, and the most absurd-yet-compelling love story of all time. The ridiculously huge primate has fallen sweetly in love with a female who is probably smaller than his penis, while the endlessly shrieking Ann fails to appreciate his passion. She's really not good enough for him. Both of the movie's remakes have had their heroines realize the depth of the beast's love, and stop screaming—trying instead to save the great doomed creature, always to no avail.

Maverick film producer Merian C. Cooper conceived this epic fantasy, and somehow persuaded RKO to spring for it. Cooper, with his writers Edgar Wallace and Ruth Rose, made Carl Denham a naked self-portrait, based romantic lead Jack Driscoll to a large degree on his partner, the film's director Ernest B. Schoedsack, while Ann Darrow was drawn from writer Rose, who was Mrs. Schoedsack.

The whole concoction is so over-the-top preposterous that it should have been laughed off the screen. But somehow it all worked, and works still. It is one of the most successful, popular, and beloved movies of all time, and deservedly so.

Although the performances of Robert Armstrong as Denham, and the charming and beautiful Fay Wray as Ann, contribute a great deal to the film's success, the person who is most responsible for making it all play was Willis O'Brien, the man who hand-animated Kong and the dinosaurs, frame by frame.

We're all familiar with the process of stop-motion animation now, but in 1933 it was a little-known technique, and audiences often didn't know how the hell the filmmakers had achieved the miraculous effects. But it wasn't just that the extinct behemoths and an absurd ape moved. O'Brien's genius lay in making Kong a real character, infusing him with a personality, a heart, and a soul. Idiotic as it seems when viewed rationally, audiences actually wept when Kong, an inanimate construct of metal, rubber and rabbit fur, gave one last longing look at his pretty pet before loosing his grip on the top of the largest phallic symbol on earth, and plummeting to Fifth Avenue far below. I confess that I have wept at that moment myself, more than once. Denham was right. It wasn't the airplanes that killed Kong. Ann Darrow broke his giant heart.

It spawned a dreadful, kitschy sequel, *Son of Kong*, which they actually had in theaters before the end of the same year *King Kong* was released. In 1949, the same team, with the addition of the great animator Ray

Harryhausen, did a kiddie-show virtual remake with a sappy, happy ending called *Mighty Joe Young*.

In 1963, Japan released the ghastly *King Kong vs. Godzilla*, a movie which took the unique approach of having two endings to its ultimate heavyweight bout. In Japan and Asia, Godzilla wins the slugfest, while in America and England, Kong is the victor.

In 1976, Dino De Laurentiis made a schlocky man-in-an-ape-suit remake that was as terrible as the original was great, and which spawned an even more abysmal sequel, the truly hilarious *King Kong Lives*. In 2005, Peter Jackson made a technically superior remake, which, while at least an hour too long, was nonetheless great fun, and respectful to the original. Sadly, Fay Wray died only a few weeks before she was scheduled to shoot a cameo appearance in the Jackson remake, to deliver the famous final line, "No, it wasn't the airplanes. It was beauty killed the beast."

6. The Invisible Man (*Universal, 1933*)

"Even the moon is frightened of me, frightened to death!"

Unlike Jules Verne, the younger H.G. Wells lived to see several of his books and stories find their way to the screen. Perhaps his two maddest scientists, Doctors Griffin and Moreau, both found their way to the screen in 1933, in Universal's *The Invisible Man* and Paramount's *Island of Lost Souls*. Moreau, on my runner-up list, made monsters. Griffin, on our top ten, became one.

The Story: A rustic Inn in the English village of Iping is visited during a howling winter snowstorm by a mysterious and ill-tempered man who wears bandages covering all of his face except his protruding nose. The man rents a room, demanding absolute privacy. As the weeks pass, he grows more irritable and rude, even assaulting the landlord. When the local constable comes to evict him, the stranger strips naked, and even hurls his fake nose at them, but his clothes seem to hold no person.

He is Dr. Jack Griffin, and in experimenting on himself he has turned himself invisible, and is now desperate to discover a way to turn visible again. Griffin enlists the aid of a co-worker, Dr. Kemp, to return to Iping to retrieve his research logs. While there, Griffin kills a police captain in full invisible view of the assembled townspeople, establishing the reality of a rampaging invisible man.

Nationwide panic ensues, while Griffin goes on a power-mad killing spree, attacking strangers, robbing banks, and wrecking a train. When Dr. Kemp betrays him to the authorities, he vows vengeance. Easily slipping past the elaborate police guards, Griffin sends Kemp off a cliff in a car. Eventually taking refuge in a barn, Griffin falls asleep. The farmer hears him snoring and reports to the police that "there's breathing in my barn." The cops surround the barn and set fire to it. When the door opens, the police fire at the approaching footprints, and the shape of a body is pressed into the snow. Later in the hospital, as Griffin dies, he regains visibility, and the moviegoing public gets its first look at Claude Rains.

When James Whale made *The Invisible Man* in 1933, Karloff was set to star, but he and Universal couldn't reach an agreement on money, so Karloff *ankled*. Colin Clive was choice two, but he was anxious to return to

THE BARELY
VISIBLE MEN

The Invisible Man was Claude Rains's screen debut, but you only glimpse him in the final shot. Several other famous faces are barely glimpsed in this picture as well. Dwight Frye is wasted in a very small role as a reporter. John Carradine does a quick bit from behind a large mustache, the formidable Violet Kemble Cooper shows up, and Walter Brennan, soon to win two Oscars, has a couple of lines in one scene.

England. Actually, he was just generally anxious. Whale knew Claude Rains from the London theater, and knew that that amazing voice was what his Invisible Man needed.

The film is a masterpiece. Often thought of as a special-effects movie, it's a rare example of an effects-heavy film where you come away thinking about the vivid characters, the compelling story, the wonderful humor, the great acting, and the striking dialogue, rather than the effects. It's always entertaining, whether stuff is floating about on wires, or empty shirts are running about singing, or hilarious Una O'Conner is just sneaking a drink or screeching.

Rains voice performance is great. He takes himself through vocal pyrotechnics he never again indulged in movies where he could be seen. He's not afraid to scream, to cackle, to run riot. His sudden outbreaks of violence are so unpredictable, so driven by a deep, mad rage, and contrast so vividly with the gentle comedy around it, that they are genuinely disturbing, even when viewed today.

7. Bride of Frankenstein *(Universal, 1935)*

"I love dead, hate living."

"You're wise in your generation."

Frankenstein had made tons of money, but it still took Universal four years to get James Whale to commit to shooting what was first called *The Return of Frankenstein*.

Whale, John Balderston, and William Hurlbut went skimming through Mary Shelley's novel and selected a few prime tidbits to build their story around. Whale kept boredom at bay by turning his horror extravaganza into a spectacular, gay black comedy, the story of a blind date between two reanimated cadavers, the biggest necrophiliac romance until *Laura*.

The Story: On a dark and stormy night, Lord Byron asks Mary Shelley to entertain him and Percy Shelley by relating what happened after *Frankenstein* ended. She tells them, "That wasn't the end at all."

The Monster survives the burning mill when he falls through the floor into a subterranean pond. Henry Frankenstein, now *Baron* Frankenstein, marries Elizabeth, but on their wedding night his old, gay professor, Dr. Septimus Pretorius, drops by and proposes jointly building a mate for the monster.

The Monster is captured by a mob, escapes, and hides out at a blind man's cabin in the woods, where he learns to speak, until passing hunters flush him out. Taking refuge in a tomb, the Monster meets Dr. Pretorius, who seduces the Monster and, when Henry gets cold feet, has the creature kidnap Elizabeth, forcing Henry to participate in the unholy project. The female creature is brought to life, but when she sees the Monster, she is repulsed. The Monster blows up the lab, killing all except Henry and Elizabeth, who escape to breed sequels.

Bride of Frankenstein is, quite simply, my favorite movie. The *fabulous* Ernest Thesiger steals the picture as Dr. Pretorius, a waspish, effeminate pouf of a Mad Scientist. Ernest was as big an old queen as ever entered a sound stage. He was a close friend of Whale's, and had already displayed his acidly camp comic persona in Whale's *The Old Dark House*. Whale wanted Thesiger for Pretorius—the role is clearly written for him—precisely to make him as overtly homosexual as he could get away with in 1935.

Thesiger, who was married, but not seriously, had once authored a book entitled *Adventures in Embroidery,* and actually used to refer to himself as "The Stitchin' Bitch." He was the companion of queens and Queens, as he was a crony of the Queen Mother, with whom he would sit, both doing needlepoint, as he amused her with his wicked gossip.

What's good about it? Everything! Script, sets, costumes, make-up, acting, photography, and, best of all, directing.

When the bride is unwrapped at the film's climax, Septimus announces "The Bride of Frankenstein." Bells

VALERIE HOBSON'S CHOICE

Follow this game of Six Degrees of Frankenstein Separation closely. In 1935, Valerie Hobson played Elizabeth Frankenstein in *Bride of Frankenstein* and Lisa Glendon in *Werewolf of London* simultaneously. Later on, after a film career that saw her play Estella in David Lean's film of Dickens's *Great Expectations* and Joan Greenwood's romantic rival in the brilliant black comedy *Kind Hearts and Coronets,* Miss Hobson married British diplomat John Profumo, who became the prime minister of England. Then, in the 1960s, Profumo was caught up in a huge scandal involving his cheating on Valerie with a party girl, a lovely euphemism for *whore,* named Christine Keeler. The scandal toppled the Profumo government. Hobson, despite the deep, almost-unfathomable public humiliation, chose to stay loyal to her husband, and never divorced him.

In the 1980s, a movie about the Profumo scandal, imaginatively titled *Scandal,* was made, in which John Profumo was played by the great, openly gay actor Sir Ian McKellan. A decade later, Sir Ian was nominated for an Oscar he should have won for playing James Whale in the great movie *Gods and Monsters,* which contained flashback recreations of Whale directing *Bride of Frankenstein*, which, to return to the start of this circle, starred Valerie Hobson, in technically the title role, since it is she who married Henry Frankenstein.

ring. The orchestra plays Rogers and Hammerstein's "Bali Ha'i" a decade before it was written, and it is all a grand, serio-comic, gothic vision of insane magnificence: the apotheosis of the Laemmles's horror visions, the summit of Whale's Everest. The most disturbing aspect of all is that, with all her scars and weirdness, the Bride, as played by Elsa Lanchester, is beautiful. Pauline Kael wrote of Elsa's Monster bride, "She won our hearts forever, as Margaret Hamilton did as the wicked witch."

Rejected once too often, the Monster reaches for the lever that will blow up the joint. (Why do they have such a lever? Does that seem like a good idea to you? What if the cat jumped on it?) Before he pulls the lever, the Bride hisses at the Monster one last time, and he looks at her with tears in his eyes. She's broken his heart, and this time, no one will fetch him a fresh one.

8. Werewolf of London (*Universal, 1935*)

"This medieval unpleasantness."

Universal's first shot at a werewolf movie was this notorious near-miss. Frankly, it wouldn't have made the top-ten list—most of the runners-up are actually better movies—but it's the *only* werewolf movie of the Golden Age.

The Story: Irritable English botanist Wilfred Glendon, while in Tibet seeking a rare flower that only blooms under the full moon, is bitten by a werewolf. Back in England, he is stalked by a mysterious Asian doctor named Yogami, who tells him that this flower is the only anecdote for the curse of the werewolf.

Glendon's bored wife, Lisa, begins seeing an old suitor, which inflames Glendon's jealousy. When the full moon rises, Glendon turns into a manbeast, and stalks the London fog, killing all he encounters.

When he tries to use his flower to stem the curse, he finds that Dr. Yogami has stolen the blooms. He confronts Yogami, who is the werewolf who bit him in Tibet, and kills him. Then he attacks his wife and her lover, but is shot by the police.

This movie, about a fierce rivalry between two werewolves who bring out the worst in each other, was written by a gay screenwriter, John Colton. Watching it, one can't help thinking how much better it would be if Boris Karloff had played Wilfred Glendon and Bela Lugosi had played Dr. Yogami.

Karloff wasn't available, as *Bride of Frankenstein* was still in production when cameras began turning on this picture. Valerie Hobson was the heroine in both and, on some days, had to shoot scenes for each of them. Warner Oland, a Swede most famous for playing Charlie Chan and Fu Manchu, here again miscast as the Asian Yogami, is kind of fun, though it's a perfect Lugosi role.

Glendon makes a natty werewolf. *After* transforming, he puts on a coat, cap, and scarf. This werewolf won't go prowling until he is properly attired and accessorized.

At one point, Glendon actually gets to say, "Lock me in. Don't open that door before sunrise. Even if I call, pay no attention to it. Keep that door locked till dawn."

You know, there's only one full moon a month on planet Earth, but the moon must have paused in its orbit in 1935, because in *Werewolf of London,* the moon is full on three consecutive nights.

The movie is poorly paced, and fails to find the pathos that would make later make Larry Talbot so memorable. This disappointing film sparked no sequels, and certainly failed to make a horror icon of dreary Henry Hull. It would be another six years before Creighton Chaney would make a werewolf the popular equal of Frankenstein and Dracula.

9. Dracula's Daughter *(Universal, 1936)*

"She was beautiful when she died a hundred years ago."

Today, when our multiplexes are cluttered with almost nothing but sequels, prequels, reboots, and re-imaginings, it may seem surprising that the Laemmles, in their entire reign at Universal, produced only two monster sequels, *Bride of Frankenstein* and *Dracula's Daughter.* Five years elapsed between *Dracula* and *Dracula's Daughter,* and between those films lay the whole of the Laemmles's horror output, for *Dracula* was their first gothic and *Dracula's Daughter* their last, actually released two months after the Laemmles's had sold the studio.

The Story: Seconds after *Dracula* ends, Van Helsing is arrested for the murder of Count Dracula. All the other characters from *Dracula* who could explain why he did it have vanished. For no reason, Van Helsing enlists a psychiatrist, Dr. Garth, to defend him instead of a lawyer. The case against him falls apart when Countess Marya Zeleska, the daughter of Count Dracula, arrives and steals her father's corpse, which she cremates in an attempt to exorcize the curse of vampirism from her family. When this fails, she implores Dr. Garth to help cure her. He mistakenly thinks she's merely insane. She then develops an unfathomable crush on the unappetizing shrink, and kidnaps his shrewish girlfriend, to force him to follow her back to Transylvania. There her jealous, evil sidekick, Sandor, kills her with a wooden arrow. It's hard to get good help.

Edward Van Sloan returns to the role of Von Helsing, bringing his same lack-of-magic to the role. Countess Marya Zeleska is lovely, sinister Gloria Holden, a felicitous piece of casting. She's wonderful in the role. Countess Zeleska's sinister sidekick, Sandor, is played by Irving Pichel. Pichel speaks in a *deep,* sepulcheral voice, always slowly and with maximum sinister intonation. If he were the voice of the telephone time clock, it would always be *too late!* Count Dracula is played by a stuffed dummy wearing a plastic Lugosi mask, who gives a more *restrained* performance than Bela was likely to have given.

Ironically, since Lugosi was originally contracted to appear in the film, but was let go when his role was reduced to just lying down and being burned—he was paid $4,000 for doing nothing—he was actually better paid than he had been on *Dracula.*

It's certainly an improvement on *Dracula.* It's better paced, it has a few effective moody scenes, particularly the scene of Zeleska cremating her dad in a spooky, foggy hollow, which has a gloriously gothic look. During the ceremony, Countess Zeleska holds, but cannot behold, a crude wooden crucifix, as she exorcizes the curse from her father.

There's a superb scene where Zaleska sits at her piano, trying to play sweet music, but with Sandor's sinister verbal interjections forcing her into a minor key, playing music that only the drinking of human blood can assuage. I have CDs like that—don't you?

But then there's Dr. Garth, and his "assistant," Janet Blake, our bickering, bantering romantic leads. Garth is supposed to be handsome, charming, and witty. Janet is supposed to be beautiful, charming, playful, and funny. Together they are supposed to have that we're-bickering-because-we-don't-know-we're-really-madly-in-love-with-each-other chemistry, and their scenes together are meant to be Noel Coward–funny. Well, she is beautiful. One out of nine isn't bad.

Kruger was fifty, and was never handsome, sexy, or charming. As cantankerous, wealthy, older men, making their heirs jump through hoops on *Perry Mason* episodes in the 1950s, he was fine. As a romantic leading man and a master of witty repartee, he is scarier than the vampires.

Churchill is very pretty, but her role is extremely annoying. When Marya says, "I am Dracula's daughter!" it's almost a surprise. I'd thought Dracula's daughter was Churchill, since she sucks the life out of every scene she's in. She and Kruger have no chemistry at all.

Much of the plot makes no sense. Having Von Helsing accused of murdering Count Dracula makes for a clever story hook, but sadly, that plotline just peters out after Dracula's corpse is stolen. Von Helsing *insists* on using Dr. Garth as his defense attorney, despite the fact that Garth isn't a lawyer. Garth, being a psychiatrist, naturally assumes that Von Helsing is insane. Given that Von Helsing has hired a doctor for a defense lawyer, and his legal defense is that "you can't murder a man who's been dead for five centuries," Garth has a point.

The film's most notorious scene is its amazing vampire-lesbian seduction. Lovely Nan Grey, who would quickly rise to more important roles, plays a girl who walks the streets at night, but isn't a prostitute because this is 1936 and the Hays Office says there's no such thing; vampires are real, but whores are a myth. She wanders out on a bridge, clearly suicidal. Sandor, lurking in the fog, a craft at which he has Olympic-level skills, steps out and tempts her with an offer to pose for an artist. Lily, appropriately named for the flower of death, agrees.

Marya is at first disappointed in Lily: "You have beautiful hands, but they're so white and bloodless." Marya plays out *the* classic lesbian, vampire seduction, quickly getting Lily out of her blouse and her bra straps down. Lily's pulsating aorta proves too much for Marya's very limited self-control, particularly when handed straight lines on a platter.

Lily: "Why are you looking at me that way? Won't I do?"

Marya: "Yes, you'll do very well indeed."

Welcome to West Transylvania, Lily.

The Laemmles had lost the studio by the time *Dracula's Daughter* opened. The new regime wanted to leave the horror business behind, so the Dracula franchise would lie dormant for seven years, before Marya's little brother would terrorize the screen.

10. Son of Frankenstein *(Universal, 1939)*

"He is my friend. He— He does things for me."

When Universal returned to making monster movies in late 1938, it was with this spectacular second Frankenstein thriller, the last great gothic fantasy of the thirties.

The Story: Many years after *Bride of Frankenstein*, Henry and Elizabeth Frankenstein's older son, Wolf, his wife, Elsa, and their excruciatingly annoying younger son, Peter, travel to the village of Frankenstein from their home in America, to claim his baronial inheritance, only to be met with hostility by the bitter villagers, and to be offered protection by sinister Inspector Krogh, whose arm was torn off by the monster when he was a boy.

Wolf also meets Ygor, a shepherd who was ineffectually hanged for body snatching. Ygor turns out to be the longtime companion of the monster, who lies comatose but alive in a tomb below the lab in which he was created. Fired with scientific zeal, Wolf revives the Monster, only to find that Ygor is sending him out to kill the surviving members of the jury that sent him to the gallows. When Wolf is accused of the murders, and the mob is howling at his gates, he kills Ygor. The Monster, crazed with grief, kidnaps Peter. Wolf and Inspector Krogh confront the Monster in the lab, and the Monster rips off Krogh's prosthetic arm. Wolf swings across the lab on a chain, and kicks the Monster into a conveniently located pool of boiling sulfur. Wolf briefly basks in the gratitude of the villagers, and then beats it out of town.

Karloff was lured back to repeat his Monster role one last time. Director Rowland V. Lee rejected the magnificent actor Peter Lorre for the titular son, and cast Basil Rathbone instead. Rathbone, happy to take the money, was otherwise dismissive of the picture. He omits any reference to *Son of Frankenstein* from his wildly egotistical autobiography.

The studio, knowing Lugosi's hunger for a role after his professional drought, cut his fee in half, and dictated that his scenes all be shot in a week. When informed of this, Lee vowed to keep Lugosi on the picture for the full production schedule, building his part way up in the process.

Added to the triumvirate of Rathbone (he receives top billing), Karloff, and Lugosi, is Lionel "Pinky" Atwill, marvelously hamming his brains out as the one-armed Inspector Krogh. (Pronounced "crow," like the bird of death.) Inspector Krogh was to become Atwill's best-remembered role.

Astonishingly, Rathbone and Atwill were both shooting *The Hound of the Baskervilles* over at 20th Century Fox *at the exact same time* that *Son of Frankenstein* was shooting at Universal.

Son of Frankenstein is well-written, well-acted by all except the cloying child "actor" Donnie Dunagan as Peter Von Frankenstein. Bela Lugosi isn't just good; he gives the best performance of his career.

Lionel Atwill tears into his role with relish, and the overacting duel between him and Rathbone is a delicious treat, top-quality scenery-chewing. With almost every line, each actor raises the acting stakes, getting more and more florid. It's great fun to watch.

HAPPY BIRTHDAY, BORIS

On November 23, 1938, in the middle of shooting *Son of Frankenstein*, Boris Karloff turned fifty-one, and the cast and crew threw him a surprise birthday party. Then the news hit the set that his wife, Dorothy, had given birth that very day to Boris's only child, Sarah Jane. According to the movie's publicity, Boris dashed off to the hospital to see his daughter without removing the Monster's green make-up.

Anyone familiar with *I Love Lucy* will recognize the plot of the episode where Ricky Ricardo dashes off to the hospital in full witch-doctor make-up for the birth of Little Ricky. It seems too good a story to be true, but then removing the Monster make-up took about an hour and a half, so it may well be a genuine fact that Boris first gazed at little Sarah Jane in his full monster face. I've spoken and corresponded with Sarah Jane, but oddly she doesn't remember her first glimpse of daddy.

The production design by Jack Otterson, though it bears no resemblance to the look of the two Whale features, is absolutely magnificent, a whole fresh gothic ambiance that really hits the Evil Fairy Tale look on the head.

Unbelievably, *Son of Frankenstein* premiered at the Pantages Theater a mere *eight days* after it completed shooting!

The Honorable Mentions

Doctor Jekyll and Mr. Hyde
(Paramount, 1931)

Fredric March won an Oscar for his energetic performance in Rouben Mamoulian's exciting version of the oft-filmed Stevenson story. Miriam Hopkins is the cockney slut Hyde can't keep his paws off. March observes his first transformation in the mirror, achieving the effect in-camera through the use of colored makeup shot through colored filters. As the filters were pulled away, Hyde's face seems to emerge. Ironically, this film is now less-remembered than the much worse MGM version of a decade later, with Spencer Tracy, Lana Turner, and Ingrid Bergman all ludicrously miscast as Londoners.

The Old Dark House *(Universal, 1932)*

James Whale's horror black comedy is a tour-de-force of gothic camp. Ernest Thesiger first trots out the arch-acid queen persona he would polish even brighter in *Bride of Frankenstein*. Melvin Douglas, Raymond Massey, Gloria Stuart, and Lillian Bond are the travelers marooned in the oldest, darkest, spookiest house in all of Wales, if not the world, during an epic storm. There they are menaced by a family, the Femms (double meaning definitely intended), who make the Addams Family look like Ozzie and Harriet, with a cackling, maniacally religious crone, Thesiger's waspishly effeminate host, a homicidal pyromaniac, Boris Karloff's mute, brutish, lust-and-booze-crazed butler, and a 102-year-old patriarch, actually played by a woman, just to put the femme in the Femms. For all its scares, it's the laughs that dominate, and you're apt to remember forever the spin Thesiger puts on lines as simple as "Please do have a po-ta-to." A nearly forgotten masterpiece.

The Mask of Fu Manchu *(MGM, 1932)*

Lavishly produced, hilarious racist claptrap, with Boris Karloff having the time of his life, camping it up as the sinister, lisping, evil genius of Sax Rohmer's pulpy novels, the embodiment of the Yellow Peril. Such MGM stalwarts as Lewis Stone and Jean Hersholt battle Fu for the golden mask and sword of Genghis Kahn, with which Fu intends to incite a race war. A young Myrna Loy plays Fu's sadistic daughter, who is excited to a sexual frenzy (I'm not kidding—a literal frenzy) watching the hunky shirtless hero being flogged, shouting "Faster! Faster!" as she does. It's idiotic and insane, but when Karloff exhorts his followers to *"Kill the white man and take his women!"* it's irresistible, though you may hate yourself in the morning.

The Mystery of the Wax Museum *(Warner Bros., 1933)*

It's a drab title, and way too much time is devoted to a laboriously unfunny "comic" subplot involving wisecracking reportress Glenda Ferrell solving the mystery, but this follow-up to Warner's earlier, inferior hit *Doctor X* has a creepy power, early two-color Technicolor photography, and stand-out performances from Lionel Atwill and Fay Wray. Wax museums are creepy enough as is, but the movie asks, What if the wax statues were actually human corpses dipped in wax? How creepy would *that* be? Mad scientist extraordinaire Atwill is here a mad sculptor. When his hands are burned in a fire and he can no longer sculpt, he begins stealing cadavers to make his wax figures. When he gets a gander at lovely Fay, he becomes as obsessed as poor old Kong did that same year, wanting to dip her in wax too, whether she's dead or not. The moment when Fay punches Lionel's face, and it *cracks* and falls off, is perhaps the best un-masking scene ever. Plus, it provided the raw material for the even better 3-D remake twenty years later that launched Vincent Price's horror career.

Island of Lost Souls *(Paramount, 1933)*

Erle C. Kenton, who later directed three of the *Franken-stein*s, directed this rare example of Paramount poach-ing Universal's horror preserve, based on H.G. Wells's horrific novel *The Island of Dr. Moreau*, and cast the im-mensely talented, gay, British actor Charles Laughton as the *very* mad scientist. *Island of Lost Souls* has literate dialogue, ghastly torture, and just drips with unsavory, overwhelmingly unnatural sex. Laughton's Moreau strides purposefully through his jungle full of mon-sters, wielding a whip with expertise and arrogance. He is God here, and he knows it and *loves* it. Laughton's per-formance is a treat. He is an education in how to over-act with skill. Lugosi, who is in the movie as one of the monsters, could have learned from him, but didn't. Laughton's Moreau is expansive, bubbling with barely

contained energy and high spirits. He is sly, mischie-
vous, tyrannical, effeminate, perverted, and intelligent,
sometimes all at once. His performance is rich, and one
can wallow in its playful fun amidst the horrors. It was
too much for 1933. It did little business domestically,
and was banned outright in England for decades, for
being "against nature." When told this, the beard of Dr.
Moreau, Elsa Lanchester, sensibly replied, "So is Mickey
Mouse." It's a potent mix, and the movie is still disturbing today, and still scary.

The Black Cat *(Universal, 1934)*

The first teaming of Karloff and Lugosi, allegedly based
on the famous story by Edgar Allan Poe, bears no trace
of resemblance to Poe's small, domestic horror story.
Instead, it's a tale of Lugosi, as a former World War I
prisoner of war, seeking revenge on Karloff's mad archi-
tect, who leads a cult of Satanists in a Bauhaus art deco
mansion built on the ruins of the prison where Lugosi
was held. They play chess for the life of the bland heroine
whom Karloff wants to sacrifice to Satan, and for good
measure, Karloff keeps his dead ex-wives vertically sus-
pended in glass cases, on display in his basement. At the
climax, Lugosi skins Karloff alive. It's a terrific, perverse
spectacle. Oh, and there's a cat in it.

The Raven *(Universal, 1935)*

My personal pick in the worst-ever-Lugosi-performance
pool. This was the second Karloff-Lugosi team movie,
and the only one where they made the error of giving
the big, florid role to Lugosi, and the smaller supporting
role to Karloff. Dr. Vollin is a mad plastic surgeon,

obsessed by Edgar Allen Poe, whom he seemed to feel needed vengeance against someone for something. From Lugosi's first appearance, unintelligibly garbling Poe' *The Raven*, Bela is off and raving. Some great acting performances are described as having "no false notes—every moment rings true." Lugosi's Vollin has no true notes. Every moment rings false. However, the extremely stupid screenplay gives him competition, and no help. Dr. Vollin is madly obsessed with a pretty dancer named Jean Thatcher. When Jean's father, Judge Thatcher, sees that Vollin is becoming obsessed by his daughter, he delivers to Bela, with a straight face, one of the stupidest lines ever written: "You don't want a young girl like Jean falling in love with you." Lugosi's curt reply a bit later in the scene, "You driveling fool, stop talking!" may be the most sensible line ever written. But there's no sense at all in Lugosi's shrieking of his climactic aria. He launches with all the force of his passionate Hungarian soul into "What torture! What a delicious torture, Bateman, greater than Poe! Poe only conceived it. I have done it, Bateman! *Poe, you are avenged!*" Followed by maniacal laughter like you've never seen, unless you've seen this movie. I'd say he was acting his brains out, but I suspect that he acted his brains out during a previous take, and that the shots in the finished film are the ones he did after his brains had gone walkabout.

Mad Love *(MGM, 1935)*

Made and released at the same time as *The Raven*, MGM's *Mad Love* has much in common with it, a *very* mad doctor obsessively in love with someone else's woman, and a wild, broad performance in the role from a passionate Hungarian actor, often required to deliver extremely silly speeches. Actor Ian Wolfe is even in both movies. It is almost as campy and funny as *The Raven*, yet it is certainly a better movie. Why? Well, it was directed by *The Mummy*'s Karl Freund, photographed by *Citizen Kane*'s Gregg Toland, and the mad doctor is the great actor Peter Lorre in his American film debut. Plus, it has Colin Clive himself, as a mad pianist. The exceptionally beautiful Francis Drake plays Yvonne Orlac, an actress who pretends to be tortured onstage every evening in Paris's *Le Théatre des Horreurs*. The World's Greatest Surgeon, Dr. Gogol, sits every evening, watching her fake torture through the narrowly parted curtains of his permanently reserved private box. As she shrieks in agony, Lorre's briefly closed eyes tells us he *enjoyed* her performance. One hopes he brought a towel. When Yvonne's concert pianist husband gets his hands crushed in a train wreck, she begs Dr. Gogol to save them. He transplants on the hands of a murderer. Gogol then launches a campaign to convince the pianist Orlac that his hands want to *kill!* Gogol buys a wax statue of Yvonne, and needless to say there's a scene at the climax where Yvonne pretends to be her own statue. Gogol is so nuts that when he notices the statue is bleeding, rather than realize it's Yvonne, he thinks he's been granted his greatest wish, that his statue has come to life, like a hot Pinocchio. *"You were wax, but you came to life in my arms . . . My love has made you live. Galatea, give me your lips."* I hope he's asking for a kiss, and not a lip transplant. *The Lips of Orlac.* "They kiss to *KILL!*"

NICE DOGGIE

In *House of Dracula*, the Wolfman never kills anyone. The first time he transforms, he's in a jail cell, and can't reach anyone. The second time he changes, he attacks Dr. Edelmann, but the moon sets in the nick of time, and he changes back before he can do anything Edelmann might regret. Why?

Since Larry Talbot, a character originally conceived by Siodmak as a someone right out of a Greek tragedy, was this time scheduled for a happily-ever-after ending, the Breen Office decreed that Larry Talbot couldn't kill anyone this time out because murderers weren't allowed to live happily ever after in the movies. Of course, the murders he'd commit weren't his fault, so he'd remain a moral innocent, and there is the question of all the people he killed in the previous three movies, but if Joseph Breen weren't an idiot, he would never have become a movie censor.

And then, in the last scene, Talbot kills Dr. Edelmann and the Frankenstein Monster, when he's in his normal persona! The Breen Office wasn't known for consistency.

The Invisible Ray (*MGM, 1936*)

Francis Drake had unfortunate taste in movie husbands. Just four months after being Colin Clive's wife and Peter Lorre's wet dream, Francis played the wife of Boris Karloff's mad Dr. Janos Rukh, in the Karloff and

Lugosi thriller, *The Invisible Ray*. Rukh is an intensely neurotic mad scientist who, like all scientists, lives in a castle, this one high in the Carpathian Mountains that looks like he bought it at Dracula's estate sale. Rukh becomes contaminated by radiation, so that he glows in the dark, very pretty, and his touch is deadly, not so pretty. Janos, whose always-shaky sanity is being eroded by the radioactive poisons in his body, decides that everyone has betrayed him, and goes about touching folks. His domineering mother practices a truly severe brand of tough love by smashing the vials of chemicals he uses to keep the radiation from burning him up. Dominating to the end, she decides when he is to die, and humiliates him in front of a crowd of people in the process. Janos, like a good son, thanks his mommy for killing him, and jumps through a second story window, bursting into a ball of fire as he does so. It's a spectacular exit from a special effects–heavy movie that is surprisingly less memorable than it sounds.

THE KING OF BLOOD:
BORIS KARLOFF (1887-1969)

"He nothing common did,
or mean, upon that
memorable scene."

The words of this Q Quote are inscribed on a plaque in St. Paul's Church, Covent Garden, in London, in memory of a British actor who was both a gentleman and a gentle man, and who achieved undying worldwide fame and affection under the self-created stage name Boris Karloff.

Of the seven supreme iconic horror stars, the Chaneys, Karloff, Lugosi, Vincent Price, Peter Cushing, and Christopher Lee, Karloff is unquestionably number one: "The King of Blood," as he refers to himself in *Targets*.

In the amazingly ongoing Karloff vs. Lugosi acting debate, the attentive reader will have long since worked out that I fall squarely into the Karloff camp. I favor Karloff over Lugosi because, based on my own viewing of a *large* number of their movies, Karloff seems to me, by far, the better actor. I have *never* seen him run riotously, over-the-top, out-of-control, on camera, as Lugosi so often did.

Not that Boris Karloff always give a great performance.

In 1958, Boris shot ten episodes of an anthology fantasy TV series for Hal Roach, called *The Veil*. Like his great later series *Thriller*, Boris hosted all the episodes, and acted in some of them. The series was never sold, never broadcast, and Boris was never paid, a fact he never forgot. It has, however, come out on DVD. In one episode, *The Crystal Ball*, Boris plays André Giraud, a charming French roué. Imagine Boris playing Maurice Chevalier's role in *Gigi*, and you have his André Giraud. He's ghastly in the part. It's a laughable embarrassment. And he was also terrible in . . . uh . . . I'm sorry, I can't come up with a second example.

Boris was born William Henry Pratt, the youngest of nine siblings, on November 23, 1887, in Camberwell, a suburb of London. Boris's great-aunt, the sister of his mother's mother, was Anna Leonowens, the Anna in *Anna and The King of Siam* and Rogers and Hammerstein's *The King and I*.

Boris's mother was half-Indian, and his Asian heritage showed in his perpetual tan. Out of make-up, Boris had very dark skin, too dark for a pleasant boyhood in conservative nineteenth-century England. His father deserting his family when Boris was five didn't help either. His mother's death, two years later, made matters still worse.

Billy Pratt, as he was known, was groomed for a diplomatic career, but he was infected with the acting bug very young, so at twenty-one he sailed to Canada to seek a theatrical career.

His earliest known film performance was in a 1919 Douglas Fairbanks film called *His Majesty, the American*. He worked off and on in films thereafter, his swarthy complexion often getting him cast as American Indians, Indian Indians, and Arabs. He was befriended by Lon Chaney, who told him, "The secret of success in Hollywood lies in being different from everyone else. Find something no one else can or will do, and they'll begin to take notice of you." Karloff certainly took this advice.

It was roles in two early classic crime melodramas, *Scarface* and *The Criminal Code*, that led to Whale casting him as the Monster in *Frankenstein*, and catapulting him to major stardom. Prior to November 1931, he was unknown. In 1932 he played the mute brute butler in Whale's hilarious black comedy, *The Old Dark House*, Sax Rohmer's Chinese super-villain in the incredibly campy, racist, MGM thriller *The Mask of Fu Manchu*, and the austere, elderly Imhotep in *The Mummy*, an unprecedented display of versatility that cemented him as Hollywood's head bogeyman.

A classic Hollywood liberal, Boris was one of the original founders of the Screen Actors Guild, holding early planning meetings in intense secrecy in his own home at, make no mistake, great personal and professional risk. His SAG membership card number had only a single digit.

Boris, like Lugosi, was married five times. In a TV interview, his only child, the charming and intelligent Sarah Jane Karloff, said in reference to the end of her parent's marriage, "I don't have the faintest clue what went wrong. But at the same time, he married my stepmother the day after the divorce was final." No, she doesn't have the *faintest* clue. That clue glares as bright as the sun.

Boris was a homebody who loved doggies, gardening, and cricket. By all accounts he was a kindly, gentle, generous man. No one who knew him ever had a bad word to say about him, except perhaps Bela Lugosi when he was in a foul mood, and Lugosi's son disputes even that. (But does one show one's nastier side to one's own son? Many a Lugosi co-star testifies to Bela's bitter assessment of Karloff.)

Along with maintaining a career as a major movie star, he regularly returned to the Broadway stage, giving acclaimed performances in *Arsenic and Old Lace, The Lark, The Linden Tree, On Borrowed Time,* and as Captain Hook in *Peter Pan.*

By the time I fell in love with Boris, he was in his final years. Fortunately, millions of my fellow Baby-Boomers were also falling for him at the time, thanks to the release of his Universal pictures to television, so his career was in its last, incandescent resurgence. He was on TV a great deal, guest-starring on variety and dramatic TV shows, and hosting the aforementioned *Thriller,* in one episode of which he co-starred with Caroline Kearney, the mother of my friend, composer, and actor Charles Bloom. Much as I loved Caroline simply for being the terrific person she was, the fact that Caroline had co-starred with Boris Karloff lifted her into my Firmament of the Awesome.

Karloff's career resurgence also resulted in fresh movies: the delightful comedies *The Raven* and *The*

Comedy of Terrors both with Vincent Price and Peter Lorre; the incoherent mess *The Terror*; the terrible H.P. Lovecraft adaptation *Die Monster, Die!*; the idiotic beach movie *The Ghost in the Invisible Bikini*; the *Man From U.N.C.L.E.* rip-off *The Venetian Affair*; the quite interesting British thriller *The Sorcerers*, and a role co-starring with his London neighbor and most-famous successor in the role of the Monster, Christopher Lee, in *The Curse of the Crimson Altar*.

Two roles that stand out on the final page of his résumé are narrating the animated TV version of Dr. Suess's *How the Grinch Stole Christmas*, a vastly better treatment of the material than the wretched Jim Carrey movie, and as horror actor Byron Orlock in Peter Bogdanovich's directorial debut, *Targets*.

In *Targets*, Boris essentially played himself, a horror star at the end of his career, feeling that the horrors of the day-to-day headlines now far eclipsed his elegant literary terrors, only to confront a psychotic sniper-killer at a drive-in playing his lame movie *The Terror*. It's a well-written, first-rate thriller and a fine, respectful coda for his career.

Only the body of Boris Karloff died on February 2, 1969. His work and his spirit will never die. In *Son of Frankenstein*, Lugosi's Ygor says to Basil Rathbone's Wolf Von Frankenstein of Karloff's Monster, "He cannot be destroyed, cannot die. Your father made him live for always." Bela never spoke truer words.

CHAPTER FOUR

The Silver Age
The Films of the 1940s

QUOTE

"Even a man who is pure
     in heart,
And says his prayers by night,
May become a wolf when
     the wolfbane blooms,
And the autumn moon is
     bright."

WITH EXTREMELY FEW EXCEPTIONS, IN THE 1940S, monsters moved into the realm of B movies. The 1943 remake of *The Phantom of the Opera* was a big-budget A picture, in Technicolor, and actually picked up two Oscars, and its rather lame Boris Karloff follow-up, *The Climax,* was also a color A release, but apart from that, the days of prestige monster movies like *Bride of Frankenstein* were over. In the forties, it was the attack of the Bs.

And so solidly was the horror market tied to war anxieties, that when the war ended in 1945, production of scary films came to a dead halt. A handful came out in 1946, but they were made in '45. After '46, there simply weren't any more. Abbott and Costello started meeting the monsters in 1948, and those films are chronicled in a separate chapter. In this chapter you will find no movies that came out later than 1946.

Universal relied on their stock monsters. In 1941, with the release of *The Wolfman,* they completed their tarot hand of monsters, and otherwise relied on sequels to extend their various monster series, and by the end of the war, were even combining them. Though their inventiveness and originality was failing, they turned steady profits.

RKO jumped on the horror hearse in 1942, when Val Lewton began producing subtler, much more literate and intelligent thrillers that creatively eclipsed Universal, but even that fresh line ground to a halt with the end of international hostilities.

Still, unlike the thirties, here I truly had to pare the list down hard to select just ten, and the sequel lines have inflated the honorable mentions as well. Quantity outshone quality during the war, but some quality managed to find it's way through. Here are the top ten, again, listed chronologically.

The Top-Ten Silver-Age Monster Movies

1. The Wolfman (*Universal, 1941*)

"The way you walked was thorny, Through no fault of your own."

Writer Curt Siodmak was a Jew born in Dresden, Germany. Having fled the Nazis under harrowing circumstances that turn his autobiography, *Wolf Man's Maker,* into a gripping read, he knew what monstrous beasts lurked within the breasts of average people. He always referred to the Nazis as Wolf People, and when he was assigned to write *The Wolf Man,* he wrote a story informed by his experience of folks who were really wolves deep inside. It's not a coincidence that the picture is full of people who are marked for death with a star, only with five points instead of six. Siodmak's timing couldn't have been more on the nose. *The Wolf Man* was released just five days after the bombing of Pearl Harbor. The full moon had risen, and the Wolf People were on a rampage.

The Story: After the death of his older son, Sir John Talbot of Wales summons home his estranged younger son, Lawrence, to prepare to assume the duties of the heir apparent to the Talbot estates and title. While on a date with village girl Gwen Conliffe to visit a gypsy encampment, Larry tries to save a young woman being attacked by what looks like a wolf, and is bitten by the animal, which he beats to death with a silver-handled cane.

The wolf was actually Bela the Gypsy in werewolf form, and the bite passes the curse to Larry. Finding himself turning into a half-man/half-wolf every evening, and killing folks, Larry is unable to convince anyone that he is guilty of the string of murders. His father becomes convinced that Larry is insane. When Gwen is attacked by the beast, Sir John beats the creature to death, only to see it transform back into his son at his feet.

The Wolf Man is a B movie that looks like an A picture, thanks primarily to a first-rate cast, including Bela Lugosi, Ralph Bellamy, acting legend Maria Ouspenskaya, Evelyn Ankers, Warren William, Patric Knowles, and the wonderful Claude Rains, fully visible now. Creighton Chaney, exploitatively billed as "Lon Chaney Jr.," has his best role since *Of Mice and Men*'s Lenny, and is excellent in the part.

It's one of Siodmak's best scripts. Siodmak is even the author of the convincingly old-sounding doggerel recited by nearly every character in the movie:

> Even a man who is pure in heart,
> And says his prayers by night,
> May become a wolf when the wolfbane blooms,
> And the autumn moon is bright.

Larry Talbot is the son of Welsh nobleman Sir John Talbot, but Siodmak, never a fan of Chaney's acting anyway, carefully established that Larry had been living in California for eighteen years. Creighton makes a convincing Californian.

Little is required of Bela Lugosi in *The Wolf Man*. He

plays a character from his own homeland, so his accent is correct. He wears little character make-up beyond a wig and a pasted-on mustache. He isn't even required to learn a new first name. He's in the film for five minutes, and he only speaks seven lines. He's good.

The movie stardom of Warren William seems inexplicable today. His Julius Caesar in DeMille's *Cleopatra*, his turn as a leading man for Mae West in *Go West, Young Man*, and his string of films as *Perry Mason* are all bewilderingly dull. His boring work in *The Wolf Man* is of a piece with these others. Ralph Bellamy, who developed into a fine actor, shows little promise of it here.

And then there's the overwhelmingly wizened old gypsy crone Maleva, played by Madam Maria Ouspenskaya. Maria's reputation as a great actress takes a beating from this tremendously camp performance. Incidentally, Maleva is supposed to be Bela's mother, but Maria was five years *younger* than Lugosi, though she certainly doesn't look it.

The Wolf Man is a good-looking film, with a particularly atmospheric foggy-forest set. Siodmak's psychological approach makes it a Greek tragedy in monster-movie guise that everyone can relate to. Gay or straight, we all have beasts within. It was a huge hit, and Larry Talbot went on to appear in four more films.

2. The Ghost of Frankenstein
(Universal, 1942)

"I made a slight miscalculation."

Remember *The Montagues*, that sequel to *Romeo and Juliet*, where those two nutty teenagers wake back up and have more adventures on their way to being united forever? No? Well, maybe that's because Shakespeare forgot to ever write it, in his hurry to get *Pericles, Cymbeline,* and *Timon of Athens* into theaters in time to qualify for the Tony Awards. But those two other star-crossed lovers, the Frankenstein Monster and Ygor did get a second shot at love, this time to be so deeply united, no man could ever tear them asunder again.

The Story: When, for no reason, the villagers of Frankenstein Village decide to dynamite Frankenstein Castle, where not-as-dead-as-he-seemed Igor is reunited with his One Great Love, when the Monster is freed from the dried-out sulfur pit. Clearly not up to par, Igor takes him to Visaria, the village where Henry Frankenstein's previously unmentioned other son, Ludwig, is treating diseases of the mind by *removing brains from people's heads, operating on them, and then reinstalling them!*

The Monster incites a near riot simply by appearing in town, but escapes from the courtroom where his sanity is being tried. Taken by Igor to Ludwig's brain clinic, he kills Dr. Kettering, a saintly assistant to Frankenstein. Ludwig decides the Monster needs a brain transplant, a perfectly reasonable treatment. Ludwig wants to put Kettering's brain into the Monster. Ygor wants his own brain used for the Monster, while the Monster makes it abundantly clear that he wants the brain of Little Chloe, a very small *girl*, placed in his skull.

Ygor wins the brain-donor pool by conning Dr. Bohmer, Frankenstein's evil assistant, played by Lionel "Pinky" Atwill, into pulling the old brain switcheroo.

Guess what? It all goes terribly wrong! Didn't see

that coming, did you? Bohmer neglects to check Ygor's and the Monster's blood types. Oops. The Monster wakes up with Ygor's voice, but blind. Of course, the mismatched blood types would actually just kill him outright, but there seems little point in complaining about one small medical error in a film full of *brain transplants*. The villagers, led by Ralph Bellamy, arrive just after the nick of time, and burn the place down. Only Bellamy, and Frankenstein's daughter Elsa, played by beautiful Evelyn Ankers, escape to go breed more sequels.

Bela Lugosi, who only three years earlier had lost his house, had just bought a new one he liked much better. Now, not only was he was returning to his best role, but Boris Karloff was 3,000 miles away, starring on Broadway in *Arsenic and Old Lace*.

With Karloff unavailable, the Universal bosses, who were unimpressed with Lugosi's, uh, versatility, went instead with Creighton Chaney for the Monster. Brilliant as Lenny, effective and even touching as Larry Talbot, he was considerably less winning in other roles. As played by Chaney, though the Monster is impressively huge, he shows little life. Only a single stony expression sits on his face, and he never emits so much as a grunt or a growl.

And then there was a problem with alcohol. Passersby the sound stages where *Ghost of Frankenstein* was shooting often saw the weird spectacle of the Frankenstein Monster slipping out the door for a quick belt from his hip flask. As the afternoons wore on, the Monster tended to become very unsteady in his giant shoes.

Ludwig is played by Sir Cedric Hardwicke. George

Bernard Shaw once told Hardwicke, "You are my fifth favorite actor, the other four being the Marx Brothers." Hardwicke was flattered by this, despite the fact that it classifies him as a lesser actor than Zeppo Marx. Cedric is solid, and his voice as always is honey, but his performance is colorless and dull.

It's really a shame they don't up take the Monster's suggestion, and give him Little Chloe's brain. The Frankenstein Monster with the developing brain of a little girl, and a little girl with the Monster's violent, criminal brain: now *that* would have made a fascinating movie: *Myra Breckenstein*!

It's a silly mess of a movie, but it's short, it's never boring, and the music is good. Ygor and the Monster, horror's Romeo and Julius, now forever united, may be dead, but if this movie has said anything, it's said that no one's death in these movies ever lasts longer than it takes to mount a sequel.

3. Cat People *(RKO, 1942)*

"I never cease to marvel at what lies behind a brownstone front."

Val Lewton ran the RKO B-movie unit in the 1940s. They had quite a unique system. The front office would invent a title, usually as lurid as they could come up with, and hand it to him, saying "Make a movie with this title, and here's your tiny budget." Lewton would then make a brilliant, shadowy, intellectual thriller that was over the heads of the studio brass.

RKO saw *The Wolf Man* rake in cash for Universal, so they enviously imagined a cat woman, and handed Lewton the title *Cat People*. Curt Siodmak wasn't specifically writing about sex when he created Larry Talbot—he was writing about Nazis—but when Val Lewton made *Cat People* over at RKO a year later, he *was* making a movie about sex, about the way that sex can awaken the beast within you, and about being terrified of awakening your beast.

The Story: Fashion designer Irena Dubrovna meets and marries a ship designer named Oliver Reed. When the wedding night comes, Irena keeps Oliver locked out of her bedroom. She's terrified of having sex with him, because she believes she will turn into a panther and eat him. When Oliver learns his wife won't have sex with him, he decides she's crazy, and sends her to a lecherous psychiatrist, who also thinks she's insane, because she won't have sex with *him*, either.

Meanwhile, Oliver blabs all of his and Irena's most intimate sexual problems to his friend at work Alice. Irena grows jealous, and Alice finds herself being stalked through Central Park and in an indoor swimming pool by some creature in the shadows that growls and screeches like a panther.

Her psychiatrist sexually assaults Irena, only to have her turn into a snarling panther in his arms. He manages to stab her with a sword before dying. She frees a real panther from the zoo next door, which kills her, while allowing the police to think the escaped beast killed the unethical shrink. Oliver and Alice marry.

The RKO brass expected a furry-faced starlet stalking himbos through the fog. When they saw the finished film, they were flummoxed. There wasn't even a monster. Lewton and director Jacques Tourneur had left it ambiguous as to whether or not Irena, the pussy person played with exquisite charm by the redundantly named French actress Simone Simon, actually turned into a panther or not. The studio insisted on inserting a panther into a few shots, but Lewton kept it in the shadows, and preserved his ambiguity.

It's intelligent, subtle, psychologically interesting, and scary. It looks great. Simone Simon is utterly charming, and much of it is just downright weird. In the justly famous sequences where Alice finds herself being stalked through the park and in a dark hotel swimming pool by something that meows menacingly, shadows and sound effects create terror out of nothing. The sure hand of director Jacques Tourneur is at work here.

This "Oliver Reed" sadly isn't the overwhelmingly sexy English actor of the same name, but rather is the spectacularly sexless and boring Kent Smith, a man somewhat less sexually exiting than overcooked tapioca pudding. Irena is convinced that if she gets sexually aroused, she'll turn into a panther and eat him, turning Oliver into food, glorious food. That she might be better off if she does never occurs to her. Jane Randolph as Alice isn't actually bad, but next to the delightful sex kitten Simone Simon, she might as well be a tree, or a scratching post.

The studio released *Cat People* with trepidation, but it was a huge hit, and Lewton made eight more brilliant, moody shockers, including *Curse of the Cat People*, which had no cat people in it at all.

4. I Walked With a Zombie (RKO, 1943)

"There's no beauty here, only death and decay."

RKO's 1943 *I Walked With a Zombie* is, in spite of the hilariously lurid title, a *great* movie, possibly the best movie discussed in this book, except for *Bride of Frankenstein*.

The Story: Naïve nurse Betsy is hired by suave Paul Holland to come to the island of St. Sebastian, to care for his wife, Jessica, who is a zombie. Betsy promptly falls in love with the morose and morbid Paul, and irrationally decides that if she can cure his wife of zombiehood, it will make him happy. She takes Jessica to a voodoo ceremony, only to discover that the voodoo priest is secretly Paul's missionary mother, Mrs. Rand. She learns that it was Mrs. Rand who turned Jessica into a zombie, as Jessica was having an affair with Paul's brother Wesley that was tearing the family apart. Jessica's condition has driven Wesley into alcoholism, and he blames his diffident brother. Learning the truth, Wesley kills Jessica to free her of the voodoo curse, and drowns himself. Everyone else lives miserably ever after.

Produced by the brilliant Val Lewton, directed by Jacques Tourneur, and written by Ardel Wray and Curt Siodmak, it's really a loose adaptation of *Jane Eyre* set in the West Indies. It features a literate screenplay, black-and-white photography so gorgeous it makes Technicolor look drab, and a fine cast, including Tom Conway as Paul, Francis Dee as Betsy, and, as Mrs. Rand, Edith Barrett, who at the time, was Mrs. Vincent Price. (Who better to be bewitching errant daughters-in-law into zombies?) An enormously tall actor named Darby Jones effectively plays a most menacing zombie stalking Betsy. There's even a maddeningly catchy calypso song about the plot, creepily performed by a genuine calypso singer named, honestly, Sir Lancelot. This is classic gothic cinema at its best.

5. Son of Dracula *(Universal, 1943)*

"I am Count Alucard. Announce me!"

According to Curt Siodmak in *Wolf Man's Maker,* much as his brother, legendary *film noir* director Robert Siodmak, and he loved each other personally, professionally they had a world-class case of sibling rivalry.

Curt had written *Son of Dracula,* and a director was needed. Curt had been supporting his brother since Robert had been fired from Paramount, for publicly referring to his product there as "Paramount shit," so Curt recommended to Universal that they assign the movie to his brother. They did. Come Robert's first day on the picture, he fired his brother. With siblings like these making the movie, is it any wonder that *Son of Dracula* is, at heart, the story of two siblings, one nice and one nasty, who come to different ends?

The Story: At Dark Oaks, a plantation somewhere deep in the American South, a party is being thrown by the Caldwell Sisters, cheery blonde Claire and morbid brunette Kay, to welcome Count Alucard, a Hungarian nobleman Kay met in Europe. Alucard is a no-show, but arrives after the festivities, killing Colonel Caldwell, the sisters' elderly father, by drinking all of his blood, though there were leftover refreshments. The Colonel's new will leaves all his money to Claire, and the plantation to Kay.

Kay then shocks her fiancé, Frank Stanley, by eloping with Alucard. Frank confronts Alucard and shoots him, but the bullet passes through him harmlessly and kills Kay, who is cowering behind him. Frank confesses to the sheriff. Kay, now a vampire herself, appears to Frank in his cell, revealing that Alucard is actually Count Dracula Jr. Kay tells Frank to kill Dracula, so that Frank and Kay can live together eternally as immortal vampires. Kay releases Frank from his cell, and he kills Alucard by burning his coffin, so the rising rays of the sun destroy him. But then Frank double-crosses Kay, burning her to death, and eradicating the curse of vampirism from America.

The Universal brass of 1943 cast Creighton Chaney as their vampire. Creighton was not an untalented actor, but he was not suited to play Count Dracula. The great actor Peter Lorre used to speak of two types of acting: acting from within, and what he called "making faces." Chaney makes many *really intense* faces at us throughout this film. Creighton here is fat-cheeked and trimly mustachioed, with sharp painted eyebrows that Divine would have killed for. He's built like a defensive linebacker, and he speaks with the voice of, well, Larry Talbot. He tries hard, but he can not rise above his miscasting. He can do menacing, but sinister is beyond his range, and suave is just plain impossible.

Kay Caldwell is played as a Southern belle with the spiffy cultured vocal tones of Mayfair, by Louise Allbritton. Kay's sister, Claire, the sunny heroine, is played by the beloved scream queen Evelyn Ankers.

Robert Siodmak gave *Son of Dracula* a wonderful, creamy-gothic look, while Curt based his story on an up-until-then overlooked idea, that to some people, vampirism has some extremely attractive attributes. It was about time that someone noticed that many people would find living on human blood a small-but-acceptable price to pay for living forever.

Robert Siodmak is quoted on the *Son of Dracula* DVD as saying, "With so little actual horror in my own life, I'm essentially a mild-mannered, gentle fellow, who feels genuinely sorry for the condemned souls characterized in movies like *Son of Dracula*." It's nice that he didn't let that Nazi Holocaust thing, which he fled Europe to survive, get him down.

Dark Oaks is the creepiest, most moss-bedecked, decaying, gothic plantation in the whole of the southern San Fernando Valley, Hell's Tara, surrounded by a sinister bayou, yet no one, I repeat, *no one at all in the entire cast,* speaks with a Southern accent. Of course, the director was a German Jew with a poor command of English. Perhaps he heard nothing unusual in having a Southern plantation inhabited by what sounds like the population of Massachusetts, visited by a Transylvanian vampire who sounds like he was from Oklahoma.

In one good scene, as Lazlo describes how a vampire can slip into a room as a vapor and listen to his enemies plot against him, Alucard slips into the room as a vapor and listens to them plot against him.

Lazlo figures out Kay's plan to deliberately become a vampire, and says that she suffers from "thanatophobia, fear of death." Do you know anyone who *doesn't* have thanatophobia? Isn't that about as common as, say, breathing?

Kay is a piece of work, deliberately inviting Dracula to her home, feeding her own father to him, marrying him, and then asking her boyfriend to kill her husband. One wonders if she's also taken out life insurance on Dracula from Fred MacMurray. If James M. Cain had ever written a gothic, Kay Caldwell of Dark Oaks would have strutted in on long legs, elegantly displayed by a slit up the side of her form-fitting shroud.

The climax, played without dialogue, is eerie and downbeat. The vampires are all dead, but the hero is going to jail for murder. It's no surprise that Robert Siodmak would go on to build a reputation for himself directing *film noir* thrillers.

6. The Uninvited (*Paramount, 1944*)

"I believe a house could be filled with malignity."

Finally the oldest monster of all, the ghost, enters our chronicle. Early Hollywood always seemed to shy away from full-out ghost stories and true haunted houses. Most ghost and haunted-house movies up to this point were comedies, and comic or serious, the hauntings tended to get explained away as bad guys lurking in secret passageways. So when Paramount decided to film a best-selling romantic ghost novel and actually leave it an unambiguous haunting, it was a groundbreaking move.

The Story: London music critic Rick Fitzgerald (Ray Milland) and his sister Pamela (Ruth Hussey) decide to buy a cliffside home, called Windward House, that they discover in Cornwall, despite it being rather a long slog back and forth to London. Windward House's owner, Commander Beech (Donald Crisp), is reluctant to sell Windward House, which has a sinister history tied to his granddaughter Stella's (Gail Russell) past.

It quickly becomes apparent that Windward House is haunted, and that the ghost seems at times to have it in for Stella, and at other times to cherish and comfort her. Rick falls quickly in love with Stella, and composes the song "Stella by Starlight" for her, but her overprotective grandfather obstructs them at every turn, and eventually has Stella committed to a mental hospital run by Miss Holloway (Cornelia Otis Skinner). Miss Holloway has a lesbian obsession with Stella's malignant dead mother, Mary Margaret, and turns Stella loose, knowing she will return to Windward House, where the ghost nearly drives her off the cliffs.

Rescued by Rick and her dying grandfather, Stella, Rick, and Pamela get to the bottom of the mystery, discovering that two ghosts haunt the house, Mary Margaret, the woman Stella believes is her mother, and her real mother, Carmel, who was her father's mistress. Mary Margaret was too selfish to sacrifice her figure to have a baby, and arranged to adopt her husband's child, only to then murder the real mother. She died trying to kill Stella, and is still determined to finish the job. Carmel's ghost has been trying to save her. With the truth out, Carmel is finally at peace, and the nasty Mary Margaret banished forever.

The relationships at the heart of this story are so twisted and complex that just boiling it down to a quick synopsis was quite difficult. The adult sexual nature of the backstory is astonishing. This is a movie from the mid-1940s in which the heroine's discovering she's a *bastard* is *good* news. Miss Holloway's lesbian obsession with Mary Margaret (a *gigantic* painting of Mary Margaret dominates her high-ceilinged office, and she basically offers up Stella as a human sacrifice to the dead woman she worships) is so severe, she makes Judith Anderson's Mrs. Danvers in Hitchcock's *Rebecca* (a film to which this picture bears more than a passing resemblance) look like a Hollywood blonde. She's the epitome of a maniac who's running an asylum.

Though mired in the limitations of the era's special effects, the picture has s spooky power. The malignant ghost's presence is signaled by a freezing cold, while Carmel's spirit's presence is signaled by the smell of mimosa. Fine acting from Milland, Crisp, and Skinner help elevate the material, and the dark, complex psychological underpinnings of the story give a weight to what might otherwise seem a bit silly. Victor Young's composition "Stella by Starlight" became a standard, and even figures into Tennessee William's masterpiece *A Streetcar Named Desire*.

For all its success, it remained a one-off. Gail Russell and director Lewis Allen attempted to recreate the magic a year later, with *The Unseen*, but it lacked real ghosts, and fizzled. It was almost twenty years before *The Innocents* and *The Haunting* brought back seriously scary big-screen ghosts.

7. The Body Snatcher *(RKO, 1945)*

The ruffian dogs, the hellish pair,
The villain Burke, the meager Hare,
Nor did they handle ax or knife,
To take away their victim's life."

When Boris Karloff returned to Hollywood after his long Broadway success in *Arsenic and Old Lace,* he made two movies, *The Climax* and *House of Franken-stein*, for Universal, neither very pleasing to him artistically, and then, his contract fulfilled, he fled to RKO and Val Lewton, and made three films in a row, all three of which make this top-ten list. And first up is this adaptation of a Robert Louis Stevenson short story. Karloff credited Lewton with "Rescuing me from the living dead, and restoring my soul." Which I take to mean he appreciated the vastly better scripts.

The Story: In 1831 Edinburgh, with the murders by the infamous body snatchers Burke and Hare still a recent memory, Dr. MacFarland (Henry Daniell) keeps his medical school supplied with cadavers procured from local graveyards by a malevolent cabbie named Gray (Boris Karloff). When grave robbing turns too difficult, Gray takes to snatching bodies that aren't all that dead yet, and speeding their departure. A dimwitted servant of MacFarland's (Bela Lugosi) makes a clumsy attempt to blackmail Gray, and shortly ends up on the dissecting slab himself. MacFarland rebels under the psychological dominance of the sadistic Gray, whose own self-esteem hinges on his control over his societal superior. The taunt of "you'll never get rid of me." drives MacFarland to murder Gray. Later, after digging up the body of a recently dead woman, during a stormy coach ride back with the corpse, MacFarland imagines that the corpse is Gray come back for revenge. His panic drives the horse to run wild, and MacFarland is killed in a crash.

This brief synopsis doesn't begin to do justice to this terrifying movie. Helmed by a master director, Robert Wise, at the dawn of his career, and produced by Val

Lewton, this is a literate, moody chiller that works up quite a head of shocks for its gruesome climax.

It also happens to be the last teaming of Karloff and Lugosi. Lewton was no fan of Bela, but the studio suggested (insisted) sticking him in for the Karloff and Lugosi marquee value. Bela is stuffed into a minor role as a very dim bulb, and for their last scene together, Boris murders Bela one last time, smothering him with one hand while he strokes his cat with the other.

But the real team here is Karloff and Henry Daniell, and they spar with superb dialogue, as Karloff's Gray wages a psychological battle for the soul of the corrupt doctor.

Like all Lewton films, there are a handful of memorable set-pieces. The aforementioned murder of Lugosi is one. In another, a mournful street singer sings plaintively as she walks into darkness under an archway. Gray's cab then follows her into the blackness. The camera just sits and stares at the dark arch, listening, until the singer's voice is suddenly cut off. And the climax, in which Karloff's pale, naked corpse seems to passively attack MacFarland, is a major blood chiller.

Bill Williams, father of future star William Katt, has a few small bits as a medical student. And there is rather a lot of singing, including the street singer's songs, and Karloff chanting the previously quoted lyrics, as he explains the *modus operandi* of Burke and Hare to Lugosi.

It's not flawless. There's a bland hero, played adequately by Russell Wade, who drags the picture down a bit in his scenes, and that always-awful, sentimental addition to any movie, an adorable crippled child whose cure necessitates several of the murders. And it does feature an Edinburgh where no one has a Scottish accent, while Lugosi, with his thick Hungarian inflection, is passed off as Spanish, but these are minor quibbles about a wonderful film.

8. The Picture of Dorian Gray. (MGM, 1945)

"If only it was the picture who was to grow old, and I remain young. There's nothing in the world I wouldn't give for that. Yes, I would give even my soul for it."

Loose talk like that can get you into trouble. It certainly lands Oscar Wilde's hedonistic, bisexual protagonist Dorian Gray in a pile of crap in both Wilde's great 1890 novel and in MGM's fine film version.

The story: In Victorian London, beautiful, narcissistic, young Dorian Gray, corrupted by the witty hedonism espoused by Lord Henry Wotton, becomes over-enamored of the huge portrait of him just painted by his friend Basil Hallward, and rashly says the words in the previous quote, in the presence of a statue of an Egyptian god, who, Wotton assures him, is fully capable of granting his wish.

Gray falls in love with an innocent young music hall singer named Sibyl Vane. Led astray by Wotton, Gray seduces Vane as a test of her purity. When she yields to him to prove her love, he rejects her as his fiancée for being a slut. She kills herself, and Gray discovers that his portrait has acquired a cruel and lustful look. He realizes that not only is his portrait aging instead of him, but each sin and crime that he commits leaves a trace in the picture, but not on him.

As the years pass, Dorian's looks never change, which inspires comments, often extremely witty comments, from his acquaintances. Dorian has sunk ever deeper into vices only vaguely hinted at, though drugs, and even bisexual dabbling, is strongly implied, and his vanity and cruelty is clearly displayed. When Gray shows the unspeakable horror that his portrait has become to Hallward, the painter is aghast. For the thrill of murder, Gray stabs Hallward, and blackmails a friend into disposing of the body. Dorian becomes engaged to Hallward's daughter, but realizing what a cruel act it would be to marry the young woman for whom he has some real feelings, he breaks off the relationship.

Returning to check on his portrait locked in his attic to see if this one act of kindness in a lifetime of decadence has shown up in the picture, he instead sees only the mocking expression of hypocrisy. Dorian stabs the painting with the same dagger he used on Hallward, only to fall dead. The painting is restored to beauty, while Dorian now wears all his sins, leaving him so disfigured, his body can only be identified by his rings.

Directors with style were a rarity at MGM, where the house style predominated, but Albert Lewin managed, and his surprisingly-faithful-to-the-book 1945 adaptation of Wilde's masterful only novel is a stylish, witty movie that is quite creepy.

Lord Henry Wotton gets all the best Oscar Wilde epigrams to deliver, such as: "Forgive me for the intelligence of my argument, I'd forgotten that you were a Member of Parliament"; "I like persons better than principles and persons with no principles better than anything at all"; and, my favorite, "It's an odd thing, but everyone who disappears is said to be seen in San Francisco. It must be a delightful city, and possess all the attractions of the next world." But it is this little zinger that sets Dorian Gray on the road to living damnation: "If I could get back my youth, I'd do anything in the world except get up early, take exercise, or be respectable."

Basil Rathbone, anxious to change his image, campaigned hard to be cast as Wotton, but it went to George Sanders, who was born to the role. Angela Lansbury, still a teenager, was extremely charming as the wronged Sibyl Vane, and was nominated for an Oscar for her performance. Sibyl is changed from the Shakespearean actress she is in the book to a music hall singer, allowing us to enjoy her delightful rendition of *Little Yellow Bird*. Hurd Hatfield brings a wonderfully curdled quality to his sleek beauty, again perfect for the role. Less perfect is Donna Reed, the *other* Miss Ellie Ewing, whose supposedly London-raised Gladys Hallward speaks as though she's from Iowa, which Reed was.

Lewin shot in black-and-white, but employed Technicolor for shock shots of the decaying portrait. The film won an Oscar for its black-and-white photography, and was nominated for black-and-white art direction. Sadly, it produced no sequels, much as I would have loved seeing *The Wallet-Sized Snapshot of Dorian Gray*. There have been a number of inferior remakes, including a trashy, Italian, openly homoerotic version in 1970, updated to the then-present, with Helmut Berger's Germanic Dorian Gray shirtless in his portrait, but it is

MGM's film and Wilde's very enjoyable read of a book that live on.

9. Isle of the Dead. *(RKO, 1945)*

"Death is good."

When ordered by the front office of RKO to make *"Isle of the Dead,* "Lewton was told by an executive named Holt, "Remember: *no* messages." Furious, Lewton replied, "I'm sorry, but we do have a message, Mr. Holt, and our message is that death is good."

Val Lewton's *Isle of the Dead* was made before and after *The Body Snatcher.* It went into production first, but after a week, Boris Karloff's chronic back problems, a lifelong leftover side effect of his early years as a lorry driver, kicked in, and production was halted. They ended up shooting *The Body Snatcher* when Boris was well enough to work again, and only after that picture was completed did filming of *Isle of the Dead* resume, some five months after it had stopped.

The Story: During the Balkan War of 1912, a plague traps a fierce Greek general, an American reporter, a British consul, his wife, her companion/nurse, and a handful of other people, on a small island used as a cemetery. Quarantined until the fast-killing plague runs its course, a superstitious old peasant woman among them begins whispering that they are really falling prey to a *vorvolaka,* a succubus-type creature that sucks the life from people, and she identifies the *vorvolaka* as the consul's wife's companion, Thea. The general decides to keep an eagle eye on Thea, just in case this old wives' tale turns out true.

The consul's wife, Mrs. St. Aubyn, also inconveniently

suffers from catalepsy, the staple disorder of Poe stories, and is mistakenly thought to be dead. She wakes up in her coffin in a crypt, and claws her way free. Now insane, she romps about the tiny island, stabbing people with a trident, and then throws herself off a cliff. The general dies before he can kill the innocent Thea. A change in the wind arbitrarily ends the plague, and the reporter and Thea, the only survivors, leave the island.

Isle of the Dead is often critically savaged. Okay, it isn't as good as most of Lewton's other thrillers. The early portions are static and talky, and the performance of Jason Robards Sr. is not up to the high standard we are used to from his supremely talented son, but compared to almost everything Universal turned out in the 1940s, it's Shakespeare. And once Mrs. St. Aubyn is interred alive, it gets seriously scary. The scene of her coffin just sitting there still while we hear her shrieks and the sounds of her fingernails frantically clawing at the wood still creeps out grown men. There are solid performances from Karloff, Katherine Emory as Mrs. St. Aubyn, and Alan Napier as Mr. St. Aubyn. (Napier, a close friend of James Whale, and best remembered today as Alfred the Butler on the 1960s TV version of *Batman,* is also in *Cat People* and *The Uninvited.*) And, like all the Lewton thrillers, it looks great.

10. Bedlam *(RKO, 1946)*

"Theirs is a bestial world, without reason, without soul; they're animals."

When I was a boy of ten or eleven, while channel-surfing one Saturday afternoon, I came across the movie *Bedlam* already in progress. I had no idea what the movie was, or what it was about, but it grabbed my attention. The film's horrifying climax has the inmates of Bedlam, thinking they have killed Master Sims, the sadistic warden of the madhouse played with chilling power by Boris Karloff, deciding to hide the body behind a half-completed brick wall, and finish the brick-laying themselves. Through the last remaining opening, we see Karloff's eyes flicker open as he regains consciousness, and registers the plight he is in. As panic starts to light up his eyes, the last brick is shoved into the hole. It scared the living crap out of me. Sleep was a long time coming that night.

The Story: In 1761 London, Nell Bowen, a woman who lives by her wits, entertaining the cloddish Lord Mortimer, becomes appalled by the inhuman conditions in which live the pitiable inmates of the St. Mary of Bethlehem Asylum for the Insane, run by Master Sims, a raving sadist with social-climbing ambitions. When she begins to challenge Sims to improve the treatment of the patients, Sims arranges for her to be wrongly committed as insane herself.

Though terrified at first, Nell makes friends among the more rational inmates, and begins helping them with little acts of kindness and care. When Sims threatens her, the inmates revolt and capture him. A kind and handsome Quaker bricklayer with a romantic interest in her helps Nell escape, while the inmates try Sims. He is found guilty of being sane, and they are on the verge of releasing him when an up-till-now catatonic woman stabs Sims with the bricklayer's trowel. The frightened inmates unknowingly wall him up alive. Later, the

Quaker lies to cover up the inmates' crime, to spare them further harsh treatment.

Talky, but with well-written dialogue, it's a serious, scary movie, that confronts genuine social issues. Anna Lee makes Nell a spirited, witty woman, more interesting than the usual horror heroine. Karloff has one of his most evil roles, and he is chilling throughout, reveling in mocking, ridiculing, and mistreating his patients, whom he regards as mere beasts.

In one frightening scene, he has his "loonies" entertain at one of Lord Mortimer's banquets, and a poor boy who has been gilded, dies trying to remember his poem, skin-poisoned like Shirley Eaton in *Goldfinger*.

The movie is scary, intelligent, and mixes the true history of the disgraceful St. Mary's Asylum with its fictional characters. It was the last of Lewton's string of literate thrillers, and it's still a nightmare-provoker.

The Honorable Mentions

The Frankenstein-Wolfman-Dracula Sequels (*Universal, 1943–1945*)

Universal combined its series as it went. The movies comprising this series are *Frankenstein Meets the Wolfman* (1943), *House of Frankenstein* (1944), and *House of Dracula* (1945).

In *Frankenstein Meets the Wolfman,* an accidentally resurrected Larry Talbot travels around Europe seeking release, accompanied by the old gypsy crone Maleva, played by the terminally campy Maria Ouspenskaya. They travel to good old Visaria, hoping that Ludwig

Frankenstein can either cure or kill Larry Talbot, where they find the Frankenstein Monster.

Creighton Chaney was originally announced to play both the Monster and the Wolfman, but after they realized what that would cost in special effects, not to mention that having an actor who was usually too drunk to work after lunch in both leads would slow production to a crawl, they wisely thought better of it. Creighton played Larry Talbot, and Bela Lugosi was miscast as the Frankenstein Monster. It's possibly Bela's worst-ever performance, although that is a hotly contested title.

In *Frankenstein Meets the Wolfman,* Lugosi is sixty years old, addicted to drugs, terribly frail, and in no physical shape even to submit to the make-up and heavy costume, let alone lug Ilona Massey around in his arms, or wrestle with Chaney's stunt double. Most of the time you're actually watching Eddie Parker play the Monster, with Bela pretty much confined to ruining close-ups.

Lugosi apologists are quick to point out that Lugosi's dialogue scenes, which established that the Monster spoke and was blind, were cut before release, thus making his staggering stiff-armed around the set, in the rare shots when it's actually Bela doing the staggering, look ridiculous. But the Monster's dialogue was cut because it made preview audiences howl with laughter. Curt Siodmak placed the blame squarely on Lugosi. Curt was even more disdainful of Bela's talent than I. He actually said that "Bela couldn't act his way out of a paper bag." I believe that, with a good script and a strong director, Bela *could* act his way out of a paper bag.

While there is no doubt that the Frankenstein Monster giving long speeches in Bela's voice would be pretty silly, I've read the scenes, and I'm afraid Siodmak must share the blame. Sir Laurence Olivier couldn't have made those scenes work.

Bela's unfortunate performance is only highlighted further by the fact that Chaney is really good in the movie. Talbot is smack dab center in his acting comfort zone, and he gives one of his best-ever performances.

When they get to the climatic slugfest between the monsters, Eddie Parker now stunt doubles Chaney, so another stuntman, Gil Perkins, doubles the Monster for the fight of whatever century this is supposed to be. Since Perkins looks nothing like Lugosi or Parker, the Monster has three easily distinguished faces in this movie. Chaney and Lugosi handled some close-ups, but otherwise sat on the sidelines, Lugosi enjoying a cigar while Chaney got drunk, as Parker and Perkins played their roles for them, until interrupted, as usual, by the killjoy village Guardians of Morality blowing up a dam that wasn't there in the last movie.

Next up was *House of Frankenstein*. Since *Frankenstein Meets the Wolfman* made a lot of money, Curt Siodmak was charged with concocting a story that would include Frankenstein's Monster, Larry Talbot, Count Dracula, a mad scientist, plus hunchbacked sinister sidekick. He knocked out something titled *The Devil's Brood* and then lit out of Universal. Curt Siodmak seldom discussed the movie afterwards, and claimed never to have seen it.

Since this would be Dracula himself again, this would be a good opportunity to return Bela Lugosi to the role. Creighton was busy playing Larry Talbot. Lugosi was available. But Universal went with John Carradine. His

Count Dracula is dapper, suave, sinister, seductive, and distinctly American. As a vampire from Albany, he'd be spiffy, but he certainly didn't sound like he'd spent much time in Romania.

Somewhere in a Europe where World War II is not raging, mad, menacing, and vicious Dr. Gustav Niemann (Boris Karloff) and his hunchbacked sidekick Daniel (J. Carrol Naish) escape from prison, and steal a traveling chamber of horrors, the central exhibit of which is the skeleton of Count Dracula.

Karloff pulls out the stake from Dracula skeleton, and his body reforms on the skeleton, including his *clothes.* For twenty minutes, Dracula causes some trouble for Peter Coe and Anne Gwynne, and then the rising sun catches him. He, *and his clothes,* fade away, and all that's left is that skeleton again.

Gustav Niemann and Daniel, looking for the infamous Frankenstein records, accidentally find Larry Talbot and the Frankenstein Monster, frozen in a subterranean ice chamber. Naturally, they thaw them out and set them free. Wouldn't you?

Once having acquired Frankenstein's notebooks, the Wolfman, the Monster, and Ilonka, a gypsy dancing girl, the gang is off to Gustav's old castle. (*Every* scientist on earth has a castle. You should see Stephen Hawking's.) Ilonka rides up front with Talbot, forming an inexplicable crush on the morose, brooding bruiser, despite his freezing rudeness. "Now don't start barking at me." she says to him, in what I hope was an intentional joke.

Up to the climax, the Frankenstein Monster, now played by the aptly named Glenn Strange, lies in the ice, lies in the show wagon, and lies on the operating table. They might as well have used Lugosi.

Once Ilonka realizes Larry really is a werewolf, he tells her, "Only death can bring us peace of mind." In the end, Ilonka proves to be a very understanding girlfriend. She shows her deep love for Talbot by killing him. She puts a lot of work into making herself a silver bullet, displaying smelting and metallurgical skills.

Grief-stricken Daniel blames Gustav for the death of Ilonka, who was killed by Talbot, and attacks him. This enrages the freshly recharged Frankenstein Monster. The Monster, and all hell, break loose. Daniel gets defenestrated. (Look it up. It only sounds dirty.)

The mob drives the Monster into a nearby swamp, dragging Gustav with him. Together they sink into quicksand. Watching fifty-seven-year-old Karloff doing his own head-going-under-the-quicksand shot, one can see why he was so overjoyed to escape from Universal to Val Lewton's smarter films over at RKO.

Sadly for the monsters, *House of Frankenstein* made a lively profit, so *House of Dracula* was inevitable. The same team, and much of the same cast, was rounded back up.

Edelmann's Creature Clinic would have made more sense as a title for *House of Dracula*, because in this movie, all the monsters come to Dr. Edelmann (Onslow Stevens) to be cured of being monsters.

Dracula, John Carradine once again, arrives first, asking to be cured of his vampirism. Okay. Now Dracula's vampirism is a supernatural curse, laid on him by Satan in return for military victories a few centuries back. Why would he seek a medical cure for a supernatural curse? Does he think Franz Edelmann is more power-ful than the ruler of hell? Come to think of it, what is he doing here at all? He and his clothes died in the previ-ous movie, yet here he and his wardrobe are, all alive and spiffy again, with no hint of an explanation. Did someone ask the children of Visaria to clap if they be-lieved in vampires?

Franz proposes a course of transfusions, or as Drac-ula usually calls them, snacks. Dr. Edelmann is such a noble doctor that he transfuses his own blood into Dracula. I've had transfusions myself, but my doctor always used *other* people's blood, the selfish bastard!

Ten minutes into *House of Dracula,* Lawrence Talbot shows up at Dr. Franz Edelmann's Clinic for the Gen-der Preference Realignment of Monsters, demanding to see him at once. How is it Larry is alive again? They don't say. Maybe Ilonka's bullet was only silver-plated.

Larry has his consultation, where his curse is X-rayed. I must share the absurd diagnosis with you: "Pressure upon certain parts of the brain. This condition, coupled with your belief that the moon can bring about a change, accomplishes exactly that. . . . When this happens, the glands generate an abnormal supply of certain hor-mones, in your case, those which bring about the physi-cal transformation which you experience." So it's all in his head. Hormones make hair sprout out of his face, change his nose into a dog snout, *and back again!* An operation using mold to soften his skull and enlarge his cranial cavity is the cure. Someone has a soft skull—I suspect screenwriter Edward T. Lowe. So how does pressure on the brain account for the way he keeps sur-viving death?

Dr. Edelmann and Larry Talbot find a dried mud flow with the Frankenstein Monster and the skeleton of Dr. Niemann poking out, in a cave beneath the clinic where he's treating Dracula and the Wolfman. *What a coincidence!* Since the Monster is comatose *again*, Edelmann starts reviving him, as killing him "would be murder." Of course, reviving him would be murder*s*. His female hunchbacked assistant and Larry Talbot talk him out of it, so the Monster is left just lying on the giant operating table that Edelmann just happens to have.

During the transfusion, Dracula uses his power of making faces to put Franz into a trance, reverses the transfusion, and *deliberately* gives Franz some of his tainted blood. This should make him a vampire, but instead it unleashes Franz's beast within, creating a Mr. Hyde semitransformation for him. Maybe pressure on his brain is unleashing hormones. It's not tied to the moon, or to a serum, or to anything. Whenever the movie needs it, Edelmann alters into a homicidal maniac.

Franz operates on Talbot, *and cures him!* Science cures a curse. I'm impressed.

He's less successful with Dracula, who has been putting the moves on his pretty receptionist, Miliza. Drac runs down to the basement. Dawn arrives two seconds after Drac closes his coffin lid. Dr. Edelmann, like all his medical predecessors in this series, tosses his "First, do no harm." oath out the window, as he drags the coffin over to the streaming sunlight and opens it. Dracula and his clothes fade away.

Although the Monster is strongly considering rousing himself off the table someday soon, Edelmann in his crazy persona nonetheless handles the hunchback-atrix's murder himself. Great, now the Monster is just watching murders.

Pinky Atwill, Larry Talbot, Miliza, and an anonymous extra cop all barge in just in time to see Nina die, and the Monster decides to join in the fun, in defense of his new boyfriend, Nutty Edelmann. The Monster hurls Pinky Atwill into an electrical apparatus and kills him in a shower of sparks, exactly the same way he killed Pinky back in *Ghost of Frankenstein*.

Talbot shoots Edelmann while the Monster just watches passively, but once Edelmann's dead, the Monster is pissed and comes for Talbot, whom he has fought before, back on their first date. Talbot knocks over some free-standing shelves and a conflagration instantly flares up. You know, if you have a lot of beakers, which, if broken, will ignite a fire so hot that it will burn down a stone room, perhaps you shouldn't store them on flimsy, free-standing shelves in the center of the room. The cat could knock it over.

The Monster flails about in footage economically lifted from the fiery climax of *Ghost of Frankenstein*, which includes close-ups of Chaney as the Monster, and long-shots of Eddie Parker, also as the Monster. That's *four* different people: Strange, Karloff (in flashbacks from *Bride of Frankenstein*), Chaney, and Parker, all seen playing the Monster in a movie in which the grand total of screen time he has doing anything but lying on a table or in a heap of mud is less than three minutes. One wonders how Fred Gwynne got left out.

The Invisible Man *Sequels* (*Universal, 1940–1944*)

The Invisible Man Returns (1940), written by Curt Siodmak, is deceptively titled, as Jack Griffin is dead. The great Vincent Price plays his first horror lead as the Invisible One, another mellifluous voice. But this time he isn't even a mad doctor. He's a man framed by Sir Cedric Hardwicke for murder. His friend, Dr. Frank Griffin, Jack Griffin's previously unmentioned brother, gives Price a shot of his brother's invisibility drug, which he happens to have lying around, to escape from prison and expose the real killer. Price is a good guy who kills nobody. The only suspense is will the drug drive him mad before he clears himself. At he end, he is cured and lives happily ever after with his girlfriend. The movie is a heavy-handed B, and despite the always-welcome Vincent Price, doesn't compare at all with Whale's superb film.

The Invisible Woman was also released in 1940, and also written by Siodmak. There is no real connection to Wells's novel at all. John Barrymore's Professor Gibbs isn't mad, just eccentric enough for a Thorne Smith novel. If you *must* have a naked woman cavorting about throughout a movie, an invisible one is the way to go. Belovedly hatchet-faced Margaret Hamilton is left visible, to engage in broad comic banter with Barrymore in this out-and-out slapstick comedy. Where else can you see the magic chemistry of *The Greatest Screen Acting Team of All Time:* John Barrymore and Shemp Howard?

Invisible Agent (1942) again finds Siodmak penning the script, with Dr. Frank Griffin, grandson of the childless Jack Griffin, using the drug to go into Germany and fight a nasty Nazi, again Cedric Hardwicke, and a sadistic Japanese Baron, played by Peter Lorre, who steals the whole film from everyone with his patented cold-blooded sadism . . . Mr. Moto as written by the Marquis de Sade. With the help of Ilona Massey, Griffin makes the world safe for freedom-loving invisible Americans everywhere. One wonders what H.G. Wells thought when he saw it. It's silly, but it moves along fast, and it's entertaining. Peter Lorre is the only real reason to see it. Jon Hall lacks both charisma and a sufficiently distinctive voice.

Nevertheless, Hall was brought back for 1944's *The Invisible Man's Revenge.* Siodmak was gone, and someone remembered that the Invisible Man should be scary, and that to do that, he must be insane. Hall's Robert Griffin, a wholly different character from the one he played in *Invisible Agent,* isn't supposed to be related to the original Jack Griffin. He just *happens* to be named Griffin. He is a revenge-crazed psychopath seeking vengeance on a snooty British family of aristocrats he thinks has wronged him. He meets John Carradine, who was in the first film, and is now a mad veterinarian making invisible pets, I guess for people with ugly doggies. The effects are more sophisticated, and if the story isn't memorable, at least he's enjoyably vicious once more. And John Carradine as a *mad vet?* Come on! That's entertainment.

The Mummy *Movies*
(Universal, 1940–1944)
The only even remotely watchable entry in the Kharis mummy series is the first, *The Mummy's Hand* (1940),

and it's terrible. The other three, *Tomb, Ghost,* and *Curse,* are so interchangeably awful that I have remained for forty years, unable to remember which title goes with which movie. When you give sequels titles like *Return of . . . , Bride of . . . , Son of . . . ,* and *Abbott and Costello Meets . . . ,* there's a clear order.

In *The Mummy's Hand,* Dick Foran plays Steve Banning, a down-on-his-luck archeologist, who, with his "sidekick" Babe Jenson, played by *Freak's* Wallace Ford, and his girlfriend Marta Solvani, played by Peggy Moran—an actress whose career spanned the era 1939 to 1942 like a pontoon bridge, just barely afloat, and then sunk without a trace—find their own temple of doom: the Temple of Karnak in the Hill of the Seven Jackals, where a living mummy named Kharis guards the tomb of the Princess Ananka. Also in the cast is George Zucco as the Evil High Priest of Karnak, Andoheb.

At the top of the movie there's a scene where the old, dying Evil High Priest passes the torch on to Andoheb. His job is to brew a tea made of "tana leaves" to feed to the living mummy Kharis, played by cowboy actor Tom Tyler, which enables Kharis to wreak the Curse of Amon-Ra, whose anger can shatter the world, on unbelievers and infidels who would dare to defile the Tomb of the Princess Ananka, Kharis's old girlfriend.

Jack Pierce put the time-consuming mummy make-up on Tyler only once, and all of Kharis's close-ups were then shot on that single day. The rest the time Tyler is wearing a rubber mummy mask. In the movie's sole effective creepy touch, in all of Tyler's close-ups, the Mummy's eyes were hand-painted, frame by frame, a solid black.

The Mummy's Hand is slower-moving than Kharis himself. To quote Addison DeWitt in *All About Eve,* the minutes fly like hours.

The sequel, *The Mummy's Tomb* (1942), came out two years later. Creighton Chaney now takes over the role of Kharis, except when Kharis was being played by stunt-man Eddie Parker, which was generally in all scenes shot after lunch. Creighton was cast solely for his name value. In fact, this is the movie in which he became billed simply as his father. Well, his father was dead, and there's no life in this role, either.

Jack Pierce didn't even bother with make-up by this time. Chaney wears a bandage suit and a one-eyed mask. Since he has no dialogue, there's simply no way to tell if it is Chaney, Parker, or Harpo Marx. One might suspect that Chaney never actually worked a day on any of his three mummy movies if it wasn't for the fact that he never stopped grousing about how much he hated the thankless, uncomfortable role. Creighton wasn't the stoic masochist his father had been.

The Mummy's Tomb is set thirty years after *The Mummy's Hand,* with Dick Foran and Wallace Ford made up to look like mummies themselves, which is more than Chaney is. The problem is, *The Mummy's Hand,* judging by the fashions, the cars, and the topical references, took place in 1940, while *The Mummy's Tomb* appears to be set in 1942.

The new Evil High Priest, Mehemet Bey, is played by the hyper-dreamy forties sex god Turhan Bey. Oh my sweet heaven, Turhan was hot. Bey is a Turkish-Czechoslovakian actor, born in Vienna, with the enormous name Turhan Gilbert Selahattin Sahultavy.

Not-quite-dead-after-all Andoheb assigns Mehemet the task of taking Kharis to Mapleton, Massachusetts, and killing all the unbelievers who defiled the Tomb of Ananka. One might wonder why Andoheb waited for thirty years to get around to doing this, since it was his only task at hand. Maybe he spent the time overfeeding Kharis, who is considerably bulkier than he was thirty years before. Chaney's Mummy has to be the only person in history to gain weight after he died. Once in America, Mehemet Bey unleashes Kharis for a killing spree. Kharis kills Steve, Babe, and Steve's sister Jane, played by the dependable Mary Gordon.

The *Mummy* movies have always been ageist, but this is a new high. *All* of Kharis's victims are senior citizens. Of course, it is worth noting that any healthy young person could outrun the slow-shuffling Mummy without breaking a sweat.

Two years later, Universal decided to resurrect Kharis once more, for *The Mummy's Ghost* (1944). Since Andoheb, Mehemet Bey, Kharis, and all the infidels who defiled the Tomb of Ananka are dead, one sees little point to it, but the Kharis pictures were made so cheaply that ten paid admissions put them in the black.

Ghost opens with basically the exact same scene both pervious films opened with: Still-not-completely-dead Andoheb recounts the backstory to his latest successor as Evil High Priest of Karnak, Yousef Bey, played by John Carradine this time, except the job is now Evil High Priest of Arkam.

Back in Mapleton, Kharis has bounced back from his latest incineration on his own, and is wandering around the Mapleton woods, looking for infidels to kill, or at least a tana bush. It turns out that local girl Amina Mansouri is the reincarnation of Princess Ananka. That's handy. It would have been quite inconvenient if it had been a girl in Cairo, Tulsa, or Reseda.

Yousef decides his mission is now to reunite the long-sundered lovers Kharis and Ananka, though if Karnak or Arkam or whoever the pertinent god is had really wanted them reunited, he had had 3,000 years in which to do it. Wasn't it their love being *forbidden* that launched the whole saga in the first place?

Amina's hair has acquired white streaks, so she looks like a cross between the Bride of Frankenstein and Cruella Deville. Her boyfriend, Tom, played by Robert Lowry, tactfully never notices.

Kharis carries Amina into one of the many quicksand-laden swamps that Massachusetts would have if it were Louisiana. On the way, Amina turns into a withered, ancient hag. Once at the bog, they sink together into the quicksand to die happily ever after, before the horrified eyes of Tom and a howling mob of villagers. It's kind of sweet, in a disgusting, necrophiliac way. For once, the Mummy gets the girl.

The next installment, *The Mummy's Curse* (1944), was released a mere five months after *The Mummy's Ghost*. It turns out that Massachusetts *is* in Louisiana, because the movie begins with the draining of the Mapleton Swamps and the uncovering of Kharis and Ananka's mummies *in Louisiana!*

Either the screenwriters forgot that the two previous movies were set in Massachusetts, difficult to believe given that *Curse* was shooting while *Ghost* was in theaters, or they thought quicksand *flowed* about 2,000 miles from Massachusetts to the Louisiana bayous, or Kharis carried Ananka in his arms, pursued by Tom and the mob of villagers, for 2,000 miles before sinking into the marsh, or no one involved with *The Mummy's Curse* gave a rat's ass about what they were doing. Which could it be? I'm stumped.

They establish that the mummy and his princess sank into the swamp *25 years ago.* That sets this movie *55 years* after *The Mummy's Hand* in 1940, yet the world, the clothes, the technology, and the social attitudes in this picture in no way resembles 1995. In fact, it looks suspiciously like 1944.

In an accidentally effective and creepy scene, Princess Ananka, the wonderful Virginia Christine, wakes up and rises out of the dried dirt of the swamp, in a shot that makes your skin crawl as much for the actress as for the character.

The characters chase each other around for forty minutes, and then Ananka reverts to a withered ancient mummy. Rather than call a doctor, the hero just states he will put her and Kharis in his museum, without so much as an autopsy for the poor, doomed girl.

One might expect that Kharis would rise yet again, as he had proved excessively resilient in the past, but we were spared that ordeal. This miserable series of movies was mercifully over, and no one was happier about that than Chaney. Sometimes dead is better.

Doctor Jekyll and Mister Hyde
(MGM, 1941)

MGM shot almost exactly the same script as Paramount's 1933 version, with Spencer Tracy, a great but quintessentially American actor, as the English Dr. Jekyll, Lana Turner, a quintessentially American, talent-free mannequin, as an upper-class English woman, and Ingrid Bergman, a voluptuous and enormously talented Swede, as a cockney slattern. The directing chores were handled by Victor Fleming, a virile, machismo-drenched, recreational hunter, best remembered for directing *The Wizard of Oz* and *Gone With the Wind*.

Spencer Tracy, in his wisdom, doesn't even attempt an accent. He plays an English Doctor living in London, one of the many Englishmen who happen to speak with a Wisconsin dialect. Lana Turner follows Tracy's lead, and then takes it a step further, attempting neither an accent nor a performance. As usual, her primary concern is displaying her wardrobe to its best advantage. Ingrid Bergman has an accent all right, one so strong she's barely intelligible, but it does not suggest she was born within the sound of Bow Bells. What it suggests is that she spent her formative years seeing the sun only six months out of every twelve. You should hear her call men "blokes."

Fleming's *Jekyll and Hyde* just sits there on the screen, presenting its weird, American England, with a Mr. Hyde who is just Dr. Jekyll grimacing with his hair overly tussled. It isn't scary, it isn't atmospheric, it isn't much of anything besides a relic of artistic hubris.

The Phantom of the Opera
(Universal, 1943)

This is a very strange movie. In 1941, Universal decided to remake its 1925 silent classic, and this Monster movie would not be a cheap little B movie, but a full-scale,

SPAWN OF DRACULA

Dracula differs from our other evil friends, Franken-stein's Monster, Larry Talbot, Imhotep, Eddie Hyde, etc., in that he actually existed. Oh, he wasn't a vampire and he didn't live for 400 years, nor was he known to wear opera cloaks, but he ruled parts of what is now Romania for three brief spans, back in the fifteenth century.

Frankly, if I had the choice of falling prey to the movies's Count Dracula or the real Vlad Dracula, a.k.a. Vlad the Impaler, I'd take the movie vampire any day. The real guy was *very* strict, and he believed in vigorous forms of corporal punishment. Running afoul of the real Dracula, by, say, stealing a loaf of bread, being a Turk, or "looking funny," could get your naughty bits snipped off, your hat nailed to your head (*ruins* the hat), your face peeled away, and then being impaled *slowly* by a huge wooden stake, while Vlad lunched nearby, enjoying the music of his screaming victims.

In both real life and reel life, Dracula was a breeder. Nasty old Vlad had three sons, though no Bub or Uncle Charlie, and Universal's Count had a daughter and a son.

Technicolor A film. They ended up spending close to $2,000,000 on it, an insanely huge amount for the time, particularly given that their biggest set was already built.

And then they decided to put the emphasis on the opera instead of on the monster. The horror in this movie wouldn't be the terror of the sinister phantom; it would be the acting and singing of Nelson Eddy and Susanna Foster. Their first choice for the heroine was Deanna Durbin, but the one small favor Heaven granted us was that Durbin refused to do the picture.

Creighton Chaney lobbied hard to be given his father's old role. The promotional value seems obvious, but the studio brass said no, and went with Claude Rains. While a fine actor, vastly better than Creighton, he nonetheless lacked the physical heft to bring any menace to the role.

Then they mucked about with the story. The phantom became a violinist fired when he can no longer play well enough, who has squandered his life savings anonymously financing the singing instruction for young Christine. Whether she is his daughter—as the movie implies but never states—or whether he has some other motivation is left murky. He has composed a musical piece, but when he mistakenly thinks his publisher has stolen it, he attacks him, and gets acid thrown in his face. Ouch!

He terrorizes the opera to further Christine's career, and drops the chandelier on the audience, after a *long* scene of his endlessly filing his way through the chain with a hacksaw, while we listen to *a lot* of opera.

I like opera, but I don't watch monster movies to be subjected to Nelson Eddy. Who did they think their audience was? This was the only horror movie my mother ever saw growing up, going only because she irrationally loved Nelson Eddy. Of course, she hated everything else about it. This is the only Nelson Eddy movie I've ever voluntarily sat through. I wanted some phantom scares, but hated Nelson, Susanna, and the movie. It has something to annoy everyone. Yet, inexplicably, it made money.

It was nominated for five Oscars: color cinematography, color art direction, music scoring and best sound, and won the first two. It's perhaps not surprising that it won for looking great, as it does, but lost for the dreary, endless music, and no one should expect to take home an Oscar for helping us *hear* Nelson Eddy.

But at least it's better than the recent Andrew Lloyd Webber version, which could almost make one nostalgic for Nelson Eddy. I said *almost*.

DIE NASTY:
LON CHANEY (1883-1930) AND
CREIGHTON CHANEY (1906-1973)

QUOTE

"Feast your eyes, glut your soul, on my accursed ugliness."

One afternoon in the 1960s, my brother Zack and I were being driven somewhere by my maternal grandfather, Cole Cleman Puett. Zack and I were in the back seat, talking to each other about the silent *Phantom of the Opera*, starring Lon Chaney, when Grampa spoke up. "Are you boys talking about the silent actor Lon Chaney?"

"Yes." I said. Then my grandfather spoke three words that forever changed how I saw him.

He said, "I knew him."

Within a minute, I was in the front seat beside him, peppering him with questions: How? When? Where? What was he like?

Grampa Puett had been a grip at MGM back in the 1920s. He had known a lot of silent stars. He'd been friends with Will Rogers. He hadn't liked cowboy star Tom Mix. I have four lovely etchings done by Lionel Barrymore I inherited from him. He got them from Mr. Barrymore when they worked together on *West of Zanzibar,* along with Lon Chaney. Grandpa Cole worked on a number of Lon Chaney's movies, though he hadn't worked on *Phantom* or *The Hunchback of Notre Dame,* as they were made by Universal.

Chaney had been a man's-man regular guy, more likely to socialize with the crew than the other actors. My grandfather seldom had a good word to say about actors, but as he reminisced about Lon that afternoon, it was clear that he not only respected Chaney, but that he had loved him.

Nowadays, thanks to DVD, most of Lon's surviving movies are readily available, and they are a revelation. Lon Chaney, one of the biggest of MGM's silent stars, was a *great* actor. It's hard for young people today, watching the broad, melodramatic, gesticulatory style of acting in silent films, to see past the almost campy overacting, but not with Chaney.

Watch *The Unknown,* with Chaney and Joan Crawford. His performance as Alonzo (Lon's real name), the Armless Knife-Thrower (yes, you read that right), will amaze you, horrify you, rip at your heart, and move you. He's *incredible!*

Watch *The Penalty,* where he plays the legless crime boss Blizzard. Blizzard's plot to conquer San Francisco with an army of anarchists is absurd (for one thing, it's tremendously hard to instill command discipline in anarchists), but Chaney's ruthless, brutal gangster out-Bogarts Humphrey Bogart. Even without Chaney's masochistic playing of the entire role on his knees, with his feet strapped to his butt (for real!), it would still be amazing.

There is a recurrent theme in Chaney's movies: unrequited love. In almost every movie, he is in love with some woman who will never love him back because, even without the grotesque make-up that was his trademark, he was no Hugh Jackman. Often it twists him into a vicious monster who plots horrible fates for his romantic rivals, but just as often, he is redeemed by his love to acts of noble self-sacrifice. In *The Unknown* he tries to have Norman Kerry's arms torn off by horses, only to throw himself under the horse's hooves to save Joan Crawford. Bette Davis might have advised him not to bother.

Time and again, through hideous make-up, a distorted body, and a long-outdated acting style, he reaches out and touches your heart. He's magnificent.

Most of the people who knew him reported glowingly of a kind and fine man. Grampa thought the world of him. But Curt Siodmak accused him of sadistic cruelty in the way he raised his son. Siodmak never met Lon. Grandpa did, so I'll take my grandfather's word.

Certainly Lon could be distant. He didn't make the Hollywood social rounds, and was happiest in a cabin he built in the mountains, far from people or roads. His first wife, Cleva, Creighton's mother, was sufficiently unhappy with him that she went to the theater where he was performing one night and drank bichloride of mercury in the stage wings. After the divorce, Lon never saw, or spoke to or of, her again.

Chaney was forty-seven and signed to play Count Dracula, when he died of throat cancer on August 26, 1930.

Creighton Chaney liked to tell the story of his being born dead in Oklahoma City in February 1906, and of his father rushing outside with his baby son in his arms, to plunge the infant into an icy river, shocking him into life. It's a great story. But Creighton also liked to tell people he had played both roles in *Frankenstein Meets the Wolfman*. Creighton liked a good story, and never let truth get in the way of one. Maybe it happened.

Lon did *not* want his son to be an actor. That Creighton would eventually find fame as Lon Chaney Jr. would have appalled Lon.

Creighton was never the great actor his father was, and that shadow was a heavy burden. But neither was he the lousy actor his worst work suggests. His performance as Lenny in *Of Mice and Men* was brilliant. Watching it, one is hard-pressed to believe this is the actor with that same face and voice who was in *The Alligator People* or *The Black Sleep*. Although mostly identified with the horror roles described in this book, he probably made as many westerns, if not more, including *High Noon*.

Testimony is very divided on Creighton as a person. Many who knew him remember a lovable, affable, regular guy, friendly, fun, and unpretentious. Ilona Massey called him, "One of the nicest, sweetest people in the world." Beverly Garland still speaks lovingly of him. Elena Verdugo remembers him "with warmth." Patricia Morrison still speaks of him as a charmer. Peter Coe became one of his best friends.

But others remember a drunken bully boy, boorish, and with his own, jock-level form of sadism. Evelyn Ankers wrote of her dislike of him in their numerous movies together, and of the nasty pranks he played on her. Jack Pierce disliked him so much that, by *House of Dracula*, he refused to make him up, and fobbed him off on an assistant. Bela Lugosi disliked him, but then disliking actors with better roles than his was Bela's trademark. Nevertheless, even Karloff never snuck up behind Bela and hoisted him aloft in the air when he was seventy-three, frail from drug rehab, and suffering from heart disease. It's doubtful that Maria Montez was too amused when Creighton pelted feces at the shingle with her name on it on her star bungalow, as reported by Siodmak in his autobiography.

Siodmak also contributes the most off-the-wall comment of all regarding Creighton. Gregory William Mank quotes Siodmak thusly: "His father dominated him to the end of his days, endangering his masculinity . . . though he raised children and was married to an understanding wife, Lon [sic] was sexually confused . . . he could not adjust to a sexual preference he was unable to accept." You know, no one likes to uncover the secret gay lives of old stars more than I, but I must emphasize that *no one else* I have interviewed or read has *ever* even hinted at such an unlikely character trait for Creighton

What no one denies was that Creighton was a drunk. Pretty much everyone who worked with him reports those liquid lunches, and Creighton's increasing uselessness on set after noon. Once can see the ravages of alcohol abuse erode his face oscreen. Look at Creighton in 1941's *The Wolf Man* and then compare his appearance with any post-1950 role. That's not just age. To quote Dame Edna, "He didn't get that nose from eating strawberries."

During the horror revival of the 1960s, American International Pictures brought Boris Karloff, Peter Lorre, and Basil Rathbone back to co-star with the divine Vincent Price, and they each made multiple pictures for the company. Creighton was also brought back by them to share Roger Corman's *The Haunted Palace* with Price. Chaney's drab performance brings little to the party. He just disappears after a while, with no story wind-up for his character at all, as though they failed to get, or had just given up trying to get, the scenes they needed from him, and he made no other picture for them, though he outlived Karloff, Lorre, and Rathbone.

He died, predictably of liver disease, on July 12, 1973. I prefer to join with those who remember him fondly. He was neither the first nor the last person to find that the liquor he consumed had consumed him. His beast within had eaten him alive.

CHAPTER FIVE

Who's on Last?

Abbott and Costello Meet the Monsters

QUOTE

"Now that we've seen the last of Dracula, the Wolfman and the Monster, there's nobody to frighten us anymore."

A LOT OF THINGS WERE OVER BY 1946. The Great Depression, from which the monsters of the thirties had diverted audiences, was long gone. World War II, whose anxieties the monsters of the forties had relieved, was over. And the Universal Studio that had made them was over as well. In 1946 it was sold again, and became the wonderfully redundant Universal-International, headed by William Goetz, son-in-law of Louis B. Mayer, held in contempt by the old MGM bastard. Goetz, a cultural snob, decreed an end to the monsters.

Abbott and Costello had made even more money for

the studio during the war than the monsters had, but they hadn't had a hit in a couple years, either, and Goetz's contempt for them was every bit the equal of his scorn for the creatures. They were headed for the pasture also. Classy, high-culture dramas were to be the new Universal-International product, which soon released *Black Narcissus, Great Expectations,* and Laurence Olivier's *Hamlet.* All fine films, but the studio was soon again verging on bankruptcy. Mayer was amused.

By 1948, the studio desperately needed something that would sell tickets, and so when producer Robert Arthur came up with the idea to combine the studio's biggest former money-makers into a single cinematic epic, Goetz gave it the go-ahead, provided they left him alone. He refused to even read the script.

Lou Costello did read the script, and hated it. Believe it or not, Abbott and Costello considered the monsters beneath them. Even after the film came out and was a huge hit, one of the top-ten grossers of the year, and one of the studio's top-three money-earners for that annum, with many a fine review as well, they still disliked it. Even though it re-established them as top stars and gave their careers a much-needed second wind, they disdained it.

When I interviewed Bud Abbott in his home in November 1972, and ventured the opinion that it was their best movie, Bud instantly refuted my assertion, insisting that their best picture was "the army picture." Bud was recovering from a stroke, which perhaps accounts for his being unable to come up with the title *Buck Privates,* despite his fervid belief that it was his best work. And perhaps *Buck Privates is* the best pure A&C film, but I still hold that *Abbott and Costello Meet Franken-stein* is overall the best movie they ever made.

Abbott and Costello Meet Frankenstein (Universal-International, 1948) is a clever, funny picture that uses the monsters for straight men to the comics, rather than as buffoons themselves. It happens that it was my introduction to these characters, as I saw it first, back around 1957 or '58.

The Story: A Mr. McDougal has acquired the remains of Dracula and the Frankenstein Monster for his Florida house of horrors, and Chic Young (Bud Abbott) and Wilbur Grey (Lou Costello) are the hapless shipping clerks who lose the exhibits. Jane Randolph, the slutty, husband-stealing Alice of *Cat People,* is the insurance investigator sent to find them.

Of course, Dracula and the monster aren't dead at all, but have wandered off after Chic and Wilbur unpack them in a sweet comic set-piece. Lugosi has finally, after seventeen years, returned to the role of Dracula. The studio insanely felt that the sixty-five-year-old Bela was too old to play the *500-year-old* Count Dracula. These people were not geniuses. It was to be Bela's last movie for a major film company.

Dracula has his own agenda going. He wants to re-animate the Monster for his own purposes, but he knows that the brain in its head is dangerously evil. He should know. As the attentive reader recalls, it's Lugosi's own brain, since it's still old Ygor's brain, considerably the worse for a lot of wear. Dracula wants a fresh, pliable brain in the Monster, and has enlisted dubious scientist Dr. Mornay (Lenore Aubert) to choose a suitable brain, and transplant it into the Monster's square skull.

Dr. Mornay, being a scientist, naturally has her own gigantic gothic castle, on an island in the Everglades, where castles are more common than alligators. There she lives with her blandly handsome assistant Dr. Stevens.

Who should also show up but Larry Talbot. His cure has worn off. Maybe his skull hardened up, and his glands went nuts once again. In any event, Miliza must have realized the obvious and left him. Or maybe he ate her. He's trailing Dracula, having appointed himself the Monster police, determined to put an end to Dracula and the Monster, and apparently over his death-wish. He does trot out that horror staple of demanding Lou lock him in his room for the night.

They keep the plot advancing, yet find time for a number of perfectly brought off comedy set-pieces. Lou sitting on the Monster's lap without noticing. Larry changing into a werewolf as he is trying to unstrap Lou from an operating table. Dracula attending a Halloween masquerade party costumed as *Dracula!*

The primary running joke is that only Lou ever sees the monsters alive. Whenever he tries to show them to Bud, they are missing in action. It's amazing how long they keep that one gag percolating.

Chaney as Talbot carries much of the picture quite well, Lugosi is excellent in his comic take on Dracula, and Glenn Strange has more to do as the Monster than in the last two movies combined. It was by all accounts a happy, fun set, with lots of onset pranks and gags, and only humorless Lugosi put off by the air of undisciplined joking going on.

The climax is a farcical, slapstick free-for-all chase.

Chaney did put on the Monster costume and make-up to double for Strange, tossing Dr. Mornay out a window when Glenn broke his foot on the first attempt.

And then, at long, long last, the monsters meet their final respective ends. Dracula, transforming into a bat to escape, is grabbed by the Wolfman, and they both plunge to the rocks and water below, while the Monster is set ablaze on a pier. Oddly, none of these deaths should work. A fall into water should not faze Dracula or the Wolfman, both of whom have survived worse, while the Monster falls through the burning pier into the water, just as he had at the beginning of *Bride of Frankenstein.*

Yet these *are* their ultimate, final deaths. seventeen years of monster fun is over. The Universal creatures have had their last hurrah. It is a glorious last hurrah. It is a vastly better movie on all levels than any of them had been in in some seven years.

The success of *Abbott and Costello Meet Frankenstein* gave new life to Abbott and Costello's careers. Over the remaining nine years of their partnership, they made six more *Abbott and Costello Meet . . .* movies, but three of them, . . . *Meet the Keystone Kops,* . . . *Meet Captain Kidd,* and the awkwardly titled . . . *Meet the Killer, Boris Karloff* (in which Karloff turned out *not* to be the killer) need not concern us here. The other three, however, were the codas to our other three major Universal monsters.

As it happens, *Abbott and Costello Meet the Invisible Man* (Universal-International, 1951) was the first movie I ever saw in a theater. On the wall of the scientist's lab is a framed picture of Claude Rains, which is little more than a respectful joke. Abbott and Costello play inept private detectives who get involved with helping an invisible boxer falsely accused of murder clear his name. A good bit of the plot of *The Invisible Man Returns* was recycled here.

It's not a very funny movie, though it's better than *Abbott and Costello Meet the Mummy,* but for chubby chasers, Lou Costello has his shirt off for the big boxing sequence, where Lou is able to pretend to box while the invisible boxer beside him does the real fighting, at least until Lou accidentally knocks his unseen helpmate out. Lou had actually been an amateur boxer in his youth, back in Paterson, New Jersey, winning thirty-two straight bouts, until a knockout ended his career in the ring.

Arthur Franz, who played the transparent fighter in *Abbott and Costello Meet the Invisible Man,* passed away during the writing of this book. We'll be seeing you, oh invisible one.

Abbott and Costello Meet Dr. Jekyll and Mr. Hyde (Universal-International, 1955) was an improvement, largely due to the casting of Boris Karloff as the sinister Victorian scientist. A lot of publicity was wrung out of Karloff's adding a new classic monster to his résumé, but actually Karloff was the first actor ever to play Henry Jekyll without also playing Edward Hyde, a record he held until 1972's *Dr. Jekyll and Sister Hyde.* At sixty-eight, he was simply too old for the athleticism the role required.

Reliable stuntman Eddie Parker played Mr. Hyde. The unsung Mr. Parker had now played the Frankenstein Monster, the Wolfman, the Mummy, and Mr. Hyde, a unique record.

No moral duality was even bothered with this time out. Karloff's Henry Jekyll was flat-out evil, while his Mr. Hyde was a bestial, subhuman creature, a monster who ran around growling, and biting people, his bites invariably turning the bitten one into another monster. Of course Lou gets bitten, and chases his partner about the Universal backlot. For the final sight gag, after killing Dr. Jekyll, Lou finds he has accidentally infected the entire police force, and Bud and Lou are chased off by a gaggle of monsters.

Abbott and Costello Meet the Mummy (Universal-International, 1955), later that same year, was nearly the last Abbott and Costello movie altogether. Kharis is renamed Klaris for no particular reason, and is played by Eddie Parker once again. The plotline, recycling the simple story of *The Mummy's Hand,* with chunks of vaudeville tossed into the mix, has a lot of tiresome running around in ancient tombs, but the formulas, both Abbott and Costello's and the Mummy's, were wrung dry by this time. Small kids, such as I was at the time, could enjoy it, but it doesn't really engage an adult viewer's attention very long. It is helped by a supporting cast that includes Marie Windsor as the slinky villainess, Michael Ansara, Dan Seymour, and a quite young Richard Deacon.

The Universal monsters were all over, and two movies later, so were Bud and Lou. The monsters were on vacation for most of the period between 1946 and 1957, when an English studio named Hammer would suddenly revive the gothic horrors to a new Technicolor world of gods and monsters.

CLOSE-UP

THE ARISTOCAMP:
VINCENT PRICE (1911-1993)

QUOTE

"A man who limits his interests, limits his life."

Abbott and Costello Meets Frankenstein was the coda for the first great wave of cinema monsters. By totally serendipitous accident, its final gag pointed a finger toward the future. Bud and Lou are paddling away in a rowboat. As they chat, they fail to notice a cigarette lighting and smoking itself. Bud says, "Oh, relax. Now that we've seen the last of Dracula, the Wolfman, and the Monster, there's nobody to frighten us anymore."

A strangely familiar, silky voice says, "Oh, that's too bad. I was hoping to get in on the excitement."

"Who said that?" barks Bud.

"Allow me to introduce myself," the voice continues. "I'm the Invisible Man."

As he laughs, Bud and Lou jump overboard and swim for shore.

The uncredited voice of the Invisible Man belongs to Vincent Price. Five years later he would make *House of Wax,* and rise from character actor to horror star. Seven years after that he would make *House of Usher,* and become *the* Great American Horror Icon of the sixties, riding the crest of the new wave of color thrillers that would come to theaters just as the Universal classics hit TV. Vincent was horror's future.

In the interests of full disclosure, I have to tell you that I *love* Vincent Price. I could just eat him with a spoon. He is one of the extremely few performers whose name alone will get me to watch a movie, no matter what it is, no matter if I know going in that it's going to stink. If Vincent Price is in it, that's reason enough for me to see it.

Once in the 1980s, I stopped at a red light on Santa Monica Boulevard a little after 2 a.m. I was in the left-turn-only lane. A car pulled to a stop to my right. Looking over, I saw that Vincent Price was driving the car. I pushed the button that lowered the window on that side of my car, and hollered as loudly as I could, *"I love you! You're wonderful!"* Vincent looked over, smiled, raised a long-fingered hand and waved. The light turned green, and he drove on towards Beverly Hills, while I turned left. It was the only time I ever saw him in the flesh. It was a golden moment: getting to scream my love to the divine Vinnie.

Vincent Leonard Price Jr. was born on May 27, 1911 in St. Louis, Missouri. His family was quite well to do. His father owned the National Candy Company. His family was a pillar of the community. Vincent exhibited a fascination with acting and theater from a very early age. After seeing John Barrymore's performance as Dr. Jekyll and Mr. Hyde, he spent hours at the mirror, making himself up as Mr. Hyde, and trying to improve on Barrymore's performance. Years later, he wrote: "Mother's suggestion that it might be more rewarding to attempt John Barrymore's Dr. Jekyll face [fell] on deaf ears. Anyone can look like John Barrymore . . . To be a wicked Roman emperor, or a dissatisfied and sinister millionaire, is much further from the truth of being a fourteen-year-old boy from St. Louis, and who wants to be fourteen in St. Louis?"

His famous interest in art began young as well. He was twelve when he began his art collection by purchasing a small Rembrandt etching with money he earned selling magazines door to door. I've had kids knock on my door selling stuff to get the money for summer camp or for their scout troops, but I've never had a twelve-year-old ring my bell and say, "Would you like to subscribe to one of these magazines? I'm trying to buy a Rembrandt." Vincent was unusual right from the start.

He grew to be six foot four, with wavy brown hair, bright blue eyes, and very handsome, with a silky voice. At seventeen, he went alone to Europe. When he returned, he went to Yale, where he was known as smart, witty, and jovial. He went to London to study for his master's degree, but there his love of theater derailed his academics. He made his stage debut in London, as a judge in a production of *Chicago*, the same play that later was adapted into the Oscar-winning musical. His second professional role was as Prince Albert in *Victoria Regina*. In 1935, the play was imported to Broadway, as a vehicle for Helen Hayes, and Price was brought along with the play. He and Helen must have looked quite the couple onstage. Price was close to two feet taller than the diminutive Miss Hayes. Future mad scientist deluxe George Zucco was also in the cast. The play was a hit, and suddenly, at twenty-four, Price was a matinee idol on Broadway.

After two years in *Victoria Regina,* Price was invited by Orson Welles to join the legendary Mercury Players. Fellow player Norman Lloyd recalled that Vincent in tights and a codpiece in Shoemaker's Holiday "served to increase our matinee business enormously." It was there that he met Edith Barrett, future star of such Val Lewton films as *I Walked With a Zombie* and *Ghost Ship,* who became the first of his three wives.

It was, appropriately enough, Universal Pictures that brought Vincent to Hollywood in 1938, where he made his screen debut in a romantic comedy called *Service Deluxe* opposite Constance Bennett, for director Rowland V. Lee, who was shortly to direct *Son of Frankenstein.* Not long after, Lee tapped him again to play Gloucester opposite Boris Karloff and Basil Rathbone in the history-as-horror film *Tower of London,* in which Karloff and Rathbone drowned him in a barrel of wine. As W.C. Fields would say, "Oh, death, where is thy sting?" He also played the title role in *The Invisible Man Returns,* which was why he was tapped for the invisible two-line cameo in *Abbott and Costello Meet Frankenstein,* but no one foresaw a horror career for him at that time, and throughout the 1940s, Price played all kinds of roles.

It is typical of his innate modesty that he invariably listed *Laura* as his best movie, a film in which he is substantially upstaged by Clifton Webb, while Dana Andrews got the girl. Price ended up with Dame Judith Anderson, which resembled getting a girl. Among other important roles in the forties were the spurned, vengeful DA in *Leave Her to Heaven,* playing opposite his great friend Tallulah Bankhead in the comedy *A Royal*

Scandal, his nasty, drug-addicted villain in *Dragon-wyck,* his first top-billed role as a homicidal psychiatrist in *Shock,* and his sublimely evil Richelieu (any hint that Richelieu was a cardinal was eliminated from the film for fear of offending the Catholic Church, history be damned) in MGM's bizarre version of *The Three Musketeers.* (Lana Turner and June Alyson as French women? Was France part of Iowa?) One can already see the scales of his casting tipping towards villains, though it was his 1941 Broadway turn in *Angel Street* that revealed his niche to him, his discovery of his ability to play what he called "the attraction of evil."

Price's career was on the upswing; Edith, now the mother of Vincent Barrett Price, wasn't doing as well. They went their separate ways, and in 1949, Vincent married his second wife, costume designer Mary Grant.

In the early fifties, he was fighting his evil image with a series of broad comic roles in *Champagne for Caesar, Curtain Call at Cactus Creek,* and *His Kind of Woman,* but then along came *House of Wax,* and all the world saw his power to chill with a chuckle, and terrify with a glance. Even after *House of Wax,* he was still making mainstream films, though his roles showed the direction he was headed: in DeMille's *The Ten Commandments* he was the lustful master builder whom Moses strangles. In *The Story of Mankind,* he went all the way to the dark side, and played the Devil himself.

He was becoming as known for his art enthusiasm as he was for his acting. He was a contestant specializing in art on the TV quiz show *$The 64,000 Challenge.* He endowed art collections, established galleries, and wrote books on art and gourmet cooking.

By the late fifties, he was making *The Fly, House on Haunted Hill, Return of the Fly, The Tingler,* and *The Bat.* Even when he played a ringmaster in *The Big Circus,* it was the most sinister circus ever. Not only was Price the ringmaster, but the clown was Peter Lorre! And sweet little David Nelson from *The Adventures of Ozzie and Harriet* played a psychopathic murderer.

But it was when Roger Corman cast him as Roderick Usher in his 1960 adaptation of Poe's *House of Usher* that the deal was sealed. Corman had been watching the success of Hammer's color gothics, and decided it was time for an American answer. Corman got American International Pictures to double his usual budget, and allow him to shoot in color. Poe was the most American of horror writers. Shooting in Panavision as well as Eastmancolor from a script by master horror novelist Richard Matheson, Corman made a very handsome, serious film very cheaply, and it was one of the three biggest hits of 1960, along with *Psycho* and *Spartacus.* Price signed a unique contract with AIP, exclusive to them for horror roles. He could make other movies for other companies, but not scary films.

For the next fourteen years, he dominated the horror field. Cushing and Lee were turning out the British thrillers, while Price was the star of seemingly every important American horror movie. Eventually Cushing, Price, and Lee would be brought together in a few films, and become great friends. He did almost every TV show on the air, becoming almost as known for his wit on *The Hollywood Squares* (over 900 episodes) as he was for his scares in the films. He was the silly Egghead on *Batman.* He did a great deal of comedy, including

The Carol Burnett Show, and such spoofy films as *Dr. Goldfoot and the Bikini Machine.*

He continued to do theater, playing the devil in *Damn Yankees,* Captain Hook in *Peter Pan,* and his acclaimed one-man turn as Oscar Wilde in *Diversions and Delights,* in which he gave 800 performances in 300 cities.

In the early seventies, as his contract with AIP was coming to an end, he did three movies that were perhaps his horror masterworks, *The Abominable Dr. Phibes, Dr. Phibes Rises Again* (with Peter Cushing), and my personal favorite of all his movies, *Theater of Blood,* where he played an insane ham Shakespearean actor who decides to kill all the London theater critics, basing each murder on one of Shakespeare's famous death scenes. It seems like such a natural idea that it's amazing no one had done it before. The role gave him a chance to play horror, black comedy, a variety of Shakespearean roles, to show the pathos of the failed actor, and yet still to suggest that the critics were right in calling his Edward Lionhart a ham. It is a masterful performance, and should have landed him an Oscar nomination.

But it landed him something he treasured more, his final wife. The Australian actress Coral Browne, beloved for her Vera Charles in *Auntie Mame,* played one of the critics he kills. They fell in love as he electrocuted her. Price was still married to Mary Grant, now the mother of his daughter Victoria, but he ended it as soon as he could, and he and Coral married, and were, by all accounts, the wittiest, wickedest, most enjoyable couple in Hollywood until Coral's death.

Vincent was known as a man who could make friends with anyone. He was beloved, and finding someone who will speak a bad word against him is a task doomed to failure. In the 1980s, his horror services were less in demand. One of his later films that I enjoy is *Madhouse,* where he plays an aging horror actor, clearly based on himself, haunted by his signature character, who seems to have come to life. Playing opposite him in *Madhouse* was Peter Cushing, and the film seems to be as much about their contrasting acting styles as it is about its plot.

If, in the eighties, he was called on to scare us in the movies less often, he was on TV every week, hosting *Mystery* for PBS. He recorded the narration on Michael Jackson's mega-hit album *Thriller.* He gave a startlingly great performance in *The Whales of August* with Bette Davis and Lillian Gish that reminded audiences one last time of what a heavyweight actor he was, when not relishing the scenery he used to chew so elegantly.

At the same time that I was falling in love with Vincent, so was another young man named Tim Burton. Burton's short animated film *Vincent,* narrated by Vincent himself, was about a boy who wanted to be just like Vincent Price, walking dark corridors, being elaborately gloomy. It's a delight. Later, Burton gave Vincent a special role as the sweet mad scientist in *Edward Scissorhands,* which amounted to a personal tribute.

Vincent died on October 25, 1993—appropriately, the week of Halloween. I wept, and so did millions of others. He was a man who shared his boundless enthusiasms with everyone, who was known for his generosity and kindness, and who, in every performance, no matter what he was playing, let us see the joy he got from acting, a contagious joy. All those who were privileged to know him seem to remember not the screams, but the laughs. To have spent time with Vincent Price was to have laughed and laughed.

Quoth the Raven, "Pull the other one." "

CHAPTER SIX

The Lead Age

The Films of the 1950s

"Keep watching the skies."

WHEN I ENTERED THE WORLD IN 1950, gothic monsters were dead in the cinema. The atomic nightmare that was Hiroshima and Nagasaki had made the anxieties of the new post-war world science-based. A handful of scientists had granted humanity, for the first time in history, the ability to actually eradicate all life on earth with just the touch of a few buttons. Hooray for science! It would not be until 1957, when England's Hammer Films would resurrect the beloved monsters of old, in sparkling new Technicolor extravaganzas, that the traditional monsters would come roaring back.

In selecting the top monster movies of the 1950s, therefore, I have had to delve into modern-dress science fiction. But since this is a book on *monster* movies, I have insisted they be movies with a monster or monsters in them. Terrifying as it was and is, *Invasion of the Body Snatchers,* for example, doesn't qualify. *The Thing From Another World* definitely does.

Here, then, are my Top-Ten Monster Movies of the 1950s, and a gaggle of Honorable Mentions.

The Top-Ten Lead-Age Monster Movies

1. The Thing From Another World (RKO, 1951)

"An intellectual carrot? The mind boggles!"

Right off we're in classic science-fiction territory, yet this great movie, with its alien vegetable creature that resembles Frankenstein's Monster, and drinks blood with all the gluttony of Dracula, is firmly rooted in the gothic monster tradition.

The Story: A mysterious, fast-moving radar blip, followed by a magnetic anomaly, leads the scientists and soldiers at the North Pole to find a flying saucer frozen in the ice. Their inept attempt to melt the ice around the saucer destroys it, but they do find its alien occupant (James Arness), which they chop out and take back to their base.

Accidentally thawed out, the alien in the ice revives, only to turn out to be a vicious killing machine. The alien is vegetable rather than animal, and feeds on animal—and *human*—blood. It begins killing the base's occupants one by one, and using their blood to nourish little things it begins growing in the base greenhouse, while a raging arctic storm prevents any escape.

A debate arises between Captain Hendry (Kenneth

Tobey), who wants to kill the thing, and Dr. Carrington (Robert Cornthwaite), who wants it kept alive for study, to learn its scientific secrets, but the debate eventually becomes moot when their struggle becomes a fight for survival. Guns and fire prove ineffective, and when its torn-off arm comes to life, it becomes clear that even dicing it would only result in making lots of little things.

Eventually, they are able to rig up a hallway to electrocute the thing, but Dr. Carrington tries to sabotage the attempt to kill it, and when this fails, he runs up to the thing, making a last try at communicating with it. The thing knocks him aside with a roar, and the men reduce it to ashes. The world is saved, but a reporter who has witnessed the whole story broadcasts a warning to the world: "Keep watching the skies."

A mystery surrounds the production of this movie. It's clearly the work of a master director. It's taut, brilliantly staged and shot. The acting is sophisticated and wonderfully paced, with dialogue overlapping just enough to suggest real conversation, but not so much that it becomes muddy or hard to follow.

Yet the credited director, Christian Nyby, an Oscar-winning editor (for *Red River*) had never directed before, and never directed another feature film. His TV work hardly suggests a master director, unless you think *Perry Mason, Mayberry RFD,* and *Gilligan's Island* are masterworks.

However the producer of the film, Howard Hawks, is one of the greatest master directors of all time, and the movie's style, look, themes, and overlapping dialogue are all hallmarks of Hawks's style. Could it be Hawks directed this picture, allowing Nyby to take the credit in order to enter the Director's Guild?

In the early eighties, I went to a party where I met Robert Cornthwaite, the wonderful actor who played the obsessed Dr. Carrington. I asked him about the directorial question, and he confirmed that Hawks rehearsed the actors, discussed each shot with Nyby, and carefully crafted the screenplay—though Charles Lederer was given sole credit, Hawks and legendary screen scribe Ben Hecht also contributed to the superb, witty screenplay—but that it was Nyby, Hawks's longtime editor, calling the shots on the set.

It can't have been a fun shoot. The scene with the saucer under the ice was shot out at the RKO ranch in the San Fernando Valley in 100-plus-degree heat, with the actors all dressed for November at the North Pole. Scenes at the base that required the actors's breath to be visible had to be shot on refrigerated sets.

Cornthwaite, who passed away during the writing of this book, and 1950s sci-fi stalwart Kenneth Tobey head a terrific cast. Margaret Sheridan makes an appealing, intelligent, superfluous heroine (the original story, *Who Goes There?*, is all-male), and the romantic banter is actually witty and fun rather than the tiresome, labored banter more often found in monster films. Some unexpected folks show up. The scientist who figures out how to kill the thing is George Fenneman, Groucho Marx's announcer-stooge on *You Bet Your Life*, and one of the other scientists is none other than the king of all voice actors, Paul Frees, in a rare on-camera role. (Both Frees and Cornthwaite showed up two years later in George

Pal's *The War of the Worlds*.) Handsome Dewey Martin, soon to be TV's Daniel Boone, is the hero's smart, wise-cracking sidekick, and, of course, James Arness, at the dawn of his stellar career, played the thankless title role.

Most science-fiction films of the 1950s are embarrassingly science illiterate. Although *The Thing* avoids the more obvious gaffes the genre was known for, it does present scientists who have collected soil samples from the North Pole, and speak of the Thing seeking out "the only open earth for miles." Actually, that should be *thousands* of miles. There is no land at the North Pole. The ice cap sits on an ocean. The book is, far more logically, set in Antarctica.

And then there is the tableful of baby things growing in their scrotal sacs. The throbbing paired pods resemble nothing more clearly that a table full of testicles. It's quite an eye-popping, disturbing image.

Despite the numerous, teeth-rattling shocks, the film is dominated by the science–vs.–military action debate. The film falls squarely on the side of the men of action who want to blast the thing back to Mars, which is hardly surprising just five years after the American Army had helped save the world from the Nazis. Twenty-five years later, in the era of *Close Encounters of the Third Kind*, a different attitude predominated.

In 1983, John Carpenter directed a spectacular remake that hewed much more closely to the novel's paranoia-infused original premise, and proved an equally scary picture.

2. House of Wax *(Warner Bros., 1953)*

"I'm going to give the people what they want: sensation, horror, shock. Send them out in the streets to tell their friends how wonderful it is to be scared to death."

Between 1949 and 1953, television went from an expensive novelty to a common household appliance, and movie attendance plummeted. Studios responded with gimmicks designed to get people off their sofas and into theaters, by offering what they couldn't get at home. Widescreen processes like Cinemascope and Cinerama, stereoscopic sound, and Technicolor were all unavailable on the crude early televisions. One of the most short-lived of these gimmicks was 3-D.

The first 3-D feature was a low-budget jungle adventure about lions eating railroad workers called *Bwana Devil.* Jack Warner was one of many who noticed that the film made a hefty profit despite being a pedantic bore. Warner decided to make the first major-studio 3-D picture, and settled on a remake of the twenty-year-old Lionel Atwill horror thriller *Mystery of the Wax Museum* for the project. It was only fitting, as the original had been one of the first color horror thrillers.

But Lionel Atwill was in his grave. A new Atwill needed to be found. Warner made an inspired choice when he offered the role to Vincent Price, then a respected character actor specializing in suave villains, but anxious to change his image and return to the Broadway stage. Price found himself forced to choose between a Broadway comedy, *My Three Angels,* and the horror movie. With regret, Price chose the film offer for its better money, and the course of horror-movie history, as well as Vincent's career, were forever changed for the better.

The Story: In turn-of-the-century New York City, gentle, refined sculptor Henry Jerrod's wax museum isn't turning a profit because Jerrod refuses to cater to sensation-seeking audiences, and put in a chamber of horrors. His grasping partner, Matthew Burke, goes for the short money from the insurance, and burns down the museum, with Jerrod in it.

A few years later, Burke is murdered by a tall, grotesquely scarred figure, who also steals Burke's body from the morgue. Next, lovely Cathy Grey is killed by the creature, and when her roommate, Sue Allen, sees the killer, he stalks her through the streets, until she takes refuge at the home of her boyfriend, sculptor Scott Andrews. Cathy's body is also stolen.

Scott interviews for a job with Jerrod, who survived the flames, but is now confined to a wheelchair, with his hands too damaged to sculpt any longer. He's employing a few sculptors to aid him in opening a new wax museum, this one filled with sensational horrors.

Visiting the new museum, Sue is shocked to see that the figure of Joan of Arc is an exact double for Cathy, right down to the single pierced ear. Jerrod in turn, is startled to see that Sue is the living double of his version of Marie Antoinette, his favorite among the statues lost in the fire. When Sue pulls the wig off of the figure of Joan of Arc, she discovers that it really *is*

Cathy, covered in wax. When Jerrod catches her in the act, he rises from his wheelchair to chase her. She punches his face, only to have it crack and fall off, revealing the scarred monster beneath. Jerrod is on the verge of coating the still-living Sue with wax when Scott and the police arrive and save her. Jerrod falls into the vat of boiling wax.

House of Wax was a big hit. Although the 3-D craze was short-lived, *House of Wax* has endured. It created the first new horror icon since Karloff and Lugosi, and, to a lesser degree, Creighton Chaney: the suave, sinister, cultured, and erudite Vincent Price.

The director, André de Toth, had only one eye, so the 3-D was lost on him, but he nonetheless packed the film with 3-D gimmick shots. Items are thrown at the viewer, fireballs explode into the audience's faces, bodies fall into the audience's laps, and in one particularly silly sequence, a paddle-ball barker smacks his rubber ball into the viewer's popcorn sack. Yet, when viewed flat, these moments do not distract from the thrills.

The plot hinges on some rather large coincidences. Two roommates, Cathy and Sue, *just happen* to be duplicates of Jerrod's earlier work, Cathy *just happens* to date Jerrod's old business partner, and Sue *just happens* to date Jerrod's next apprentice.

More problematic is the fact that it is *obvious* that the maniacal monster stalking and killing, plainly seen from early on, is Jerrod right from the start. Thick as the make-up is, Price is still recognizable in it, and his height and bearing is also unmistakable, so the big revelation that Jerrod is the monster is no revelation at all.

The scenes of Jerrod stalking Sue go on way too long. The sequences of the police investigation also take up too much screen time. There's a long scene in a music hall shot on the saloon set built for *Calamity Jane.* The scene appears to be included for no other reason than to allow a row of 3-D can-can girls to kick their legs above the audience's heads, and thrust their bloomered butts into the viewer's faces.

Phyllis Kirk is rather dull as Sue, and Frank Lovejoy is also uncharismatic as the police inspector, and inexplicably receives second billing. Carolyn Jones, as usual, is charming as the ditzy Cathy. Paul Picerni, the last of the film's principals to survive today, is handsome and sexy as the hunky, young sculptor, Scott, although he has little to do. A young Charles Bronson is suitably menacing as a mute sculptor named Igor. Dabbs Greer is lively and likable as the inspector's brighter sidekick. Paul Cavanagh, once an unappetizing leading man for Mae West in her *Goin' to Town,* makes a bland art patron. Both Kirk and Greer passed away during the writing of this book, scant weeks apart.

But for all its defects, the basic premise of a wax museum that is full of wax-coated cadavers is still potent. Many of the shock scenes are quite effective, and the scenes of burning and melting human figures in the prologue's conflagration sequence is extremely gruesome and creepy.

However, its real power lies in Vincent Price's smooth, layered performance. It is a star-making turn, and really shows off the goods that were to power his amazing run of star horror roles in the 1960s and '70s.

3. The Beast From 20,000 Fathoms
(*Warner Bros., 1953*)

"I feel I am leaving a world of untold tomorrows, for a world of countless yesterdays."

Ray Harryhausen's *The Beast From 20,000 Fathoms* is probably the least of the movies on this top-ten list, but it was tremendously influential, spawning a whole subgenre of giant-beast and/or dinosaur monster movies, including every Godzilla picture ever made, and remained the best of its ilk.

The Story: "Operation Experiment" (someone must have sat up all night coming up with that title), an above-ground nuclear-bomb test, is held somewhere off Baffin Bay, north of the Arctic Circle. The irresponsible scientists performing this reckless experiment will soon learn just how dangerous it is, as their blast thaws out and revives a carnivorous, amphibious dinosaur. One scientist, Tom Nesbitt, sees the beast, but can not convince anyone else of its reality.

The beast heads south towards its old mating ground, which is now the island of Manhattan. Along the way it sinks boats and wrecks a lighthouse. Finally, with the help of a survivor of one of the attacks, Nesbitt convinces Professor Elson, "the foremost paleontologist in the world," that the monster is real. Elson goes looking for it in a diving bell, finds it, and is promptly eaten by it.

Now that there is proof of the monster's existence, it becomes moot, as the monster comes ashore in Manhattan, and wreaks havoc on the city. Its blood proves to carry a virulent prehistoric disease bacteria that is killing more people than the beast itself. Cornered at last in a Coney Island roller coaster, an army sharpshooter shoots an atomic isotope into a wound in the beast's throat. This poisons the creature, while also destroying the deadly bacteria in its bloodstream.

The story is almost simpler than my synopsis. There is a sort of romance going on between Nesbitt and Professor Elson's secretary, Lee Hunter, but the film doesn't insist too hard on it.

There's an unintentionally funny scene when a psychiatrist, played by King Donavon, comes to interview Nesbitt. Nesbitt's doctor tells him the shrink "wants to ask you a few questions." The shrink then sits down, and without asking even a single question, and ignoring what very little he allows Nesbitt to say, proceeds to tell him why he hallucinated the whole thing. He arrives with his diagnosis complete before he even meets the patient. Sadly, there is no later scene of the shrink learning how wrong he is, preferably by getting stepped on or eaten by the beast.

The dialogue scenes are all flat and poorly written There are no interesting characters, but the encounters with the beast—when it attacks a fishing boat and when it wrecks a lonely lighthouse—have beauty and power, and the last twenty minutes are spectacular.

Professor Elson, played with charm by Cecil Kellaway, announces in his first scene that he's about to take his first vacation in thirty years. By the law of movie clichés, this means he's *doomed!* Sure enough, at the instant of his greatest personal and professional triumph, he's eaten by the monster.

Several familiar faces pop up. Nesbitt's doctor is

Frank Ferguson, who had just appeared in *House of Wax*. He's also the proprietor of the house of horrors in *Abbott and Costello Meet Frankenstein*. Kenneth Tobey, scant months after saving the world from the Thing, plays a nearly identical role as an army colonel. Lee Van Cleef makes his screen debut as the sharpshooter who kills the beast. James Best, very young and very skinny, appears unbilled in the opening scenes. In the trailer for the film, a then-unknown Vera Miles and *House of Wax*'s Paul Picerni make quick appearances, though they are not in the film itself.

Nesbitt is played by Swiss-born actor Paul Christian. In his informative and lavishly illustrated autobiography, Ray Harryhausen writes of Christian, "I always thought it sad that Christian never managed to 'make it' in movies, as I considered him a fine and believable actor who turned in an engaging performance." It must not have occurred to Ray to fact-check his statement. *The Beast From 20,000 Fathoms* was Christian's twenty-third movie. He returned to Europe where, under his real name, Paul Hubschmid, he appeared in over seventy more movies, eventually being honored for his services to German cinema, where he was a major star.

The dinosaur is called a Rhedosaurus. It was invented for the movie, and is far larger than any carnivore that ever really lived. Ray Harryhausen stoutly maintains that his monster's invented name starting with Ray's own initials is just a coincidence. Whatever you say, Ray.

We will cut Ray Harryhausen slack because his amazing and beautiful work is what makes this picture a billion times superior to the best Godzilla movie ever made. He brings his beast to breathing life, and we end up feeling for the poor monster, awakening to a world far different from the world he left, hounded and eventually killed for merely following his instincts. His bewilderment and fear can be felt, even as he waddles through Manhattan, eating anyone who gets too close. If he's not exactly King Kong, he's still a tortured, innocent animal.

And Ray did his work on a truly tiny budget. He invented techniques for combining his images that saved thousands of dollars, which was fortunate because this independently made movie had no money to spend. Brought in for around $200,000, the producers sold it to Warner Bros. for $400,00, and congratulated themselves on a 100 percent profit. Then Warner Bros. released it, and it made millions. Oops. Ray admits in his book that he actually lost money on the film, but counts it a plus for all he learned and invented making it. It was his first solo feature effort, and marked the beginning of one of the most amazing careers in film history.

By coincidence, it was his only professional work with his lifelong best friend, Ray Bradbury. Bradbury wrote a science-fiction short story about a lonely dinosaur that mistakes the foghorn of an isolated lighthouse for the call of its mate. When it finds no lady dinosaur, it destroys the lighthouse, and dies of a broken heart. The story was published in the *Saturday Evening Post,* and the producers of *The Beast From 20,000 Fathoms* helped themselves to it. Then they thick-headedly brought

Bradbury in to consult on the script. He read it and pointed out its similarities to his own published story, and went home. The producers immediately bought the rights to the story and title. Both Rays still enjoy good chuckles retelling that tale.

Every dinosaur to trample a city since owes its genesis to this movie, but few of them possess its simple pleasures.

4. Creature From the Black Lagoon (*Universal-International, 1954*)

"There are many strange legends in the Amazon. Even I, Lucas, have heard the legend of a man-fish."

Producer William Alland, perhaps best remembered for his acting turn as the reporter assigned to find the meaning of *"Rosebud"* in *Citizen Kane*, was the man producing Universal-International's string of 1950s science-fiction programmers. His best-loved films—*It Came from Outer Space, Tarantula*, and *The Incredible Shrinking Man*—are rooted firmly in post-war sci-fi interests and anxieties. His 1954 *Creature From the Black Lagoon*, however, though also undeniably science fiction, created the last entry into the Universal gothic monsters pantheon, ironically swimming into existence just as its older siblings were having their final bouts opposite Abbott and Costello. It was conceived by Alland himself, from equal parts of Sir Arthur Conan Doyle's *The Lost World* and a shaggy-fish story he heard over dinner one evening of a supposedly real Amazonian half-man/half-fish with a letch for human ladies. Almost without realizing it, they tapped into the fears of anyone who has ever swum in murky open waters, while wondering what might be lurking deep below, the same fears that were later successfully milked by Steven Spielberg in *Jaws*.

The Story: The discovery of a fossilized fish-hand-claw in an Amazonian tributary inspires an American scientific research team to take an expedition up the tributary into *The Black Lagoon*! The team includes David Reed (Richard Carlson), his girlfriend, Kay Lawrence (Julia Adams), and the money man Mark Williams (Richard Denning), who lusts for Kay.

Kay, who has apparently never heard of piranha, goes for a relaxing swim in the Black Lagoon, where she arouses the lusts of the gillman, an evolutionary dead-end man-fish lurking in the depths below. David wants to catch and study the creature, while Mark, always preening to show Kay how much more macho than David he is, wants to kill it and bring it home stuffed.

Environmentally oblivious, they dump enormous quantities of a poison into the lagoon, which successfully kills all the fish, and brings a groggy gillman to the boat. They follow the creature back to its cave lair, which is nicely lit for a cave, and take it prisoner.

The sight of Kay on deck drives the gillman to break out of its flimsy cage. It attacks Dr. Thompson (Whit Bissell) before diving overboard. They decide to get Thompson to a medical facility. Their escape is foiled however, when they find the lagoon exit has been barricaded by the creature, who has now turned the tables and taken *them* prisoner. As they clear the logs from their way, the creature, after killing Mark, comes aboard and steals Kay, taking her to his cave lair. David finds her there, but is attacked by the creature. The ship's captain and the sole remaining uninjured scientist shoot the creature several times, and it staggers back to its lagoon, to drift to the bottom, apparently, but not definitely, dead.

Alland's successful previous film, *It Came From Outer Space,* based on a Ray Bradbury story, had been shot in 3-D, so Alland decided to make *Creature* the very first underwater 3-D movie. This creates a rather weird effect. Rather than immersing the audience underwater, it presents the viewer with what appears to be a huge cube of gray water (the movie is in black-and-white) floating in front of him. Having seen this film both flat and in 3-D, I think it works better flat.

Alland's usual director, the stylish yet efficient Jack Arnold, gives the film plenty of menace and action. It profits from the helpless feeling of being in an environment where one can move only sluggishly, pitted against a foe perfectly adapted to the conditions. Beloved by all fans of this movie is Kay's famous swimming scene, with her sailing gracefully along the surface, while the creature swims beneath her, facing up, an underwater ballet of menaced innocence and lust.

The whole film is powered by sexual tensions: first, the lust of the creature for Kay is a motor under the whole plot; second, the sexual rivalry between David and Mark keeps the plot moving when the creature's away.

Given that the two leading men spend more than half the movie shirtless, and usually in tight, wet swim trunks, it's unfortunate that they went with Richard Carlson and Richard Denning. Rock Hudson and Tab

Hunter would have provided more eye-candy than just Julie Adams, who certainly looks fetching in her once-piece bathing suits.

The creature is played by two performers. Big Ben Chapman plays the gillman out of water, while the shorter, slimmer professional diver Ricou Browning does all the creature's underwater scenes.

The picture was a big hit, and spawned two sequels. The first, *Revenge of the Creature* (1955), also shot in 3-D, featuring a wholly different cast apart from Browning as the swimming gillman (the topside gillman this time was Tom Hennesey), was basically an aquatic remake of *King Kong*. A second expedition captures the creature and takes it to Florida's Marineland (a real aquarium, where much of the film was shot), to be put on public display. It escapes, kidnaps the heroine (this time Lori Nelson), and wreaks havoc, until hero John Agar rescues her, and the creature heads out to sea, apparently intending to swim all the way back to the Amazon. Clint Eastwood plays a very brief early scene with a chimp.

In the third, *The Creature Walks Among Us* (1956), shot flat, yet another expedition again captures the gillman, but in the process burns it's gills so badly it could die. They find it also has lungs, so an operation is performed to activate its lungs, turning it into a land creature, and making it much bulkier, as the post-operation creature is played by Don Megowan, who was nearly twice as wide as Ricou, who still played the swimming creature. They bring it back to a facility near San Francisco, but once again a set of three-way sexual tensions enrage the creature, whose violent passions are aroused by the sight of human violence. He goes berserk, breaks loose, kills off the bad guy, and returns to the ocean and an uncertain fate.

Yet perhaps the creature will walk among us once more, as a remake of *Creature From the Black Lagoon* is in production as I write.

Forbidden Planet *(MGM, 1956)*

"My evil self is at that door, and I have no power to stop it!"

Forbidden Planet is hard-core, space-opera science fiction. It looks for all the world like an episode of *Star Trek* a decade early. But its invisible monster from the id places it squarely on our monster movie list.

The Story: In the twenty-second century, a flying saucer from earth arrives at the fourth planet orbiting the star Altair, to rescue the space explorers of the ship *Belleraphon,* who landed there twenty years earlier, and haven't been heard from since. Over the radio, the voice of Dr. Morbius (Walter Pidgeon) warns them not to land. Altair 4, it seems, is—gulp!—*Forbidden*!

They land anyway, and find that Dr. Morbius and his daughter, Altaira (Anne Francis, for those of you who have never seen *The Rocky Horror Picture Show*), born on the planet, are the only survivors of the *Belleraphon.* All the others were murdered by a mysterious planetary force within a few months of their landing.

Altaira has never seen a man before, and wants to learn about kissing, with the all-male crew more than ready to give her instructions. Rather quickly, though, she falls in love with Captain John Adams (Leslie Neilson). Also making a friend is the ship's cook, (Earl

Holliman), who gets Morbius's servant, Robby the Robot (Marvin Miller), to manufacture him gallons of whisky.

An invisible force begins killing crew members. The crew erects an electronic fence, which reveals a grotesque, otherwise-invisible monster that is ripping crew members apart.

Morbius takes the captain and first officers underground and shows them a vast machine, twenty miles cubed, the last remaining relic of the Krell, the superior civilization that once inhabited the planet, now extinct for two million years, which enabled the Krell to exist without instrumentation. He also shows them a machine that boosted his own intelligence above any known human level.

At the sacrifice of his life, the ship's physician, Dr. Ostrow (Warren Stevens), subjects himself to the brain-boosting machine, and, as he dies, reveals the planet's secret to Adams. The Krell had invented a machine that read their minds and manufactured whatever they wanted, "creation by mere thought." But they hadn't reckoned on their own primitive instincts, and the monsters from their ids, their own Mr. Hydes, ran riot. As Nielson describes it: "The secret devil of every soul on the planet, all set free at once to loot and maim, and take revenge, Morbius, and *kill*"—wiping out the entire civilization in a single night of terror.

Since Morbius had boosted his brain, the Krell machine had begun functioning on his thoughts. When the crew of the *Belleraphon* voted against Morbius to return to earth, the Krell machine had tapped into his unconscious anger and made a monster from his id that killed all the crew. Now that Adams's ship has landed against his wishes, his unconscious fury against them has again summoned up a monster from the id to kill them. Only when this is explained to Morbius himself, does he confront his inner demon and refute it, destroying the monster, and dying himself in the process. At his dying instruction, Adams activates the button that will blow up the planet, and he, Altaira, Robby, and the other survivors leave for earth.

This complex, adult mystery, a combination of Freudian psychology and Shakespeare's *The Tempest* dressed up as a kid's colorful space adventure, makes for a potent mix. There are the usual 1950s sci-fi scientific gaffes. The film opens with a narrator, Les Tremayne, informing us that mankind landed on the moon "in the last decade of the twenty-first century"; they were only off by 130 years. Morbius says how the machine's control panel makes him wish he "had multiple arms and legs"; not being an amputee, he *has* multiple arms and legs. In his living room hangs a "futuristic" light fixture identical to the one hanging in my parent's dining room the year the film was made.

MGM spent money, making an A film to compete with the many low-budget, black-and-white, sci-fi exploitation movies in the theaters of the era, and struck box-office gold. It looks familiar now, even to people who have never seen it, because MGM reused so much from it. The space crew's uniforms were used in many a *Twilight Zone* episode. Alan Young even shows up in one in a scene in George Pal's 1960 *The Time Machine*. The Krell power meters showed up as props countless times, and even the flying saucer was reused on a number of episodes of *The Twilight Zone* as well. Robby the Robot made so many subsequent appearances in films and on television that it became a star of sorts also.

The appearance of the invisible monster from the id in the force-field fence was cartoon animation done by Joshua Meador, borrowed from Walt Disney for the sequence. Disney Studios is credited in the opening titles. A lot of publicity was centered on the omnipresent electronic, futuristic, musical score by Luis and Bebe Barron, but I'm afraid it's a horrible cacophony of noises that makes for a most unpleasant soundtrack in an otherwise very enjoyable picture.

In the 1970s, when asked about *Forbidden Planet* by interviewer Stephen Rebello, Walter Pidgeon's only comment was "Was I in that thing?" Anne Francis, Leslie Nielson, and Warren Stevens, however, remain proud of it. When I found myself sitting next to Earl Holliman at a Dame Edna stage show last year, he was only too happy to chat about this fondly remembered movie.

Part of its cult status certainly results from MGM having the wisdom never to make *Return to the Forbidden Planet*. It remains an entertaining and intelligent one-off.

6. The Curse of Frankenstein *(Hammer, 1957)*

"I always had a brilliant intellect."

And then came Hammer. Gothic monsters were dead on the screen in the 1950s. Grade-Z-level exploiters like

Blood of Dracula (1957) and *Frankenstein 1970* (1958) dressed up monsters that looked little better than a child's Halloween costume, and set them tottering through tired paces in modern dress. And then two things happened: Some of the classic Universal monster movies of the 1930s were released to television, and in May, 1957, just three weeks before the death of James Whale, Hammer Films released its groundbreaking Technicolor gothic *The Curse of Frankenstein* starring Peter Cushing and Christopher Lee, and everything changed.

The Story: In Switzerland in 1860, a priest visits a condemned prisoner. The prisoner, Baron Victor Frankenstein (Peter Cushing), begs the priest to listen to his tale and intercede to halt his impending execution.

Single-minded, egotistical Victor tells of how he and his tutor-turned-assistant, Paul (Robert Urquhart), conducted experiments in the resurrection of the dead. Victor decides to construct an artificial human from dead bodies, and grant life where it has never been. Paul is revolted, but reluctantly goes along at first.

Elizabeth (Hazel Court), Victor's ward, arrives, convinced she is his fiancée, unaware that Victor is having an affair with the upstairs maid, Justine (Valerie Gaunt). Paul grows ever more repulsed by Victor's grave-robbing, but remains to protect Elizabeth. Victor invites elderly Professor Bernstein, "the greatest brain in Europe," to dinner, and kills him. Paul catches Victor in the crypt, stealing the professor's brain. They fight, and the jar containing the brain gets smashed. Victor spends hours picking the glass out of the brain, hoping it's still usable.

Victor brings the creature (Christopher Lee) to life, and its first act is to try and kill Victor, who is saved only by Paul's timely arrival. The next day Victor and Paul find the creature has escaped the lab into the surrounding woods.

The creature encounters an old blind man and a little boy in the woods and kills them both. When Victor and Paul catch up to the creature, Paul shoots it dead, and they bury it in the woods.

Victor digs the creature up and brings it to life a second time, now making an effort to teach its damaged brain (which was crushed by a fall off a balcony, smashed full of glass in the jar, and now shot in the face—that is one heavily damaged brain) to obey simple commands.

Justine, now pregnant, tries to blackmail Victor into marrying her instead of Elizabeth. Victor locks her in the monster's cell, and the look on the monster's face at the fade-out implies that the monster rapes her before killing her.

Victor weds Elizabeth. When Paul arrives for the reception, Victor shows him the restored monster, now exhibiting the responses of a severely retarded child. Elizabeth goes snooping in the lab just as the creature breaks loose. Victor rushes upstairs to save Elizabeth. He throws a lamp at the monster, setting it on fire, and the creature plunges through a glass skylight and into a conveniently placed vat of acid, utterly destroying its body.

The priest is unimpressed with the blasphemous story. Paul and Elizabeth also refuse to corroborate Victor's tale, so Victor is led off to the guillotine for the murder of Justine.

You may have noticed a certain problem with this story. Victor, very much an atheist, is telling a priest this story of wild blasphemy to clear his name of the crime of murdering Justine, who was killed by the monster when Victor locked her in with the monster *in order for the monster to kill her.* Plus, the story contains a confession to the cold-blooded murder by Victor of Professor Bernstein, as well as a lot of grave-robbing and bribery. As exculpatory testimony goes, it's pretty inept. And the "good people," Paul and Elizabeth, perjure themselves to help send Victor to his death. Nice folks. There's really no reason for them to lie. The truth is more than sufficient to get Victor executed, a fact Victor clearly fails to appreciate.

The terribly superior Baron simply drips with attitude. He seems to have spent as much time studying sarcasm as anatomy. Victor kills Professor Bernstein by pushing him off a balcony to land head first on a marble floor below, *in order to steal his brain,* although a method of homicide *not* involving massive brain damage might seem a better tactic. When the monster turns out to be—*Surprise!*—brain damaged, Victor blames Paul. But while the shards of glass in the brain certainly didn't do it any good, neither did *smashing it on a marble floor.* The Baron's resurrecting the monster again after Paul shoots him makes the last twenty minutes of the film seem like its own sequel.

Hammer Films, a tiny outfit, turning out five low-budget films per year, and shooting at a manor house near Windsor that they were calling Bray Studios, had tried cashing in on the fifties sci-fi fad with a few black-and-white science-fiction films of their own, from the silly *The Four-Sided Triangle* to the excellent *X, the Unknown* and *The Creeping Unknown (The Quatermass Xperiment),* the latter you will find in our Honorable Mentions. These films had done quite well. The heads of Hammer, Anthony Hinds and Michael Carreras, had noticed that *The Creeping Unknown* had contained a monster, with critics comparing Richard Wordsworth's performance favorably to Boris Karloff's performance as the Frankenstein monster.

They decided to risk upping the budget to do a costume, period monster movie in Technicolor, featuring Peter Cushing. who, though unknown in America, was a big TV star in England. Terence Fisher, who had directed *The Four-Sided Triangle,* was tapped to direct, and Jimmy Sangster to write, this all-new approach to Mary Shelley's story.

Along with being the first gothic in color, it pushed the taste envelope on gore, being far more gruesome than anything made by Universal, with Technicolor to really make the blood pop. But the gorgeous cinematography also emphasized the handsome period settings, the beautiful costumes, and Peter Cushing's bright blue eyes.

The dialogue has bite and wit, and Peter Cushing's fine acting elevates the picture, and indeed *every* movie he graces, even extremely dumb piles of crap like *At the Earth's Core* and *Doctor Who and the Daleks.* Like every real star, watching him play *anything* is a pleasure.

Lee's monster, owing to copyright issues, looked nothing like Karloff's, but to my eyes, seemed more to resemble the monster I imagined when I read the book, a patchwork quilt of a man, right down to his mismatched eyes. His staggering, pathetic creature was more pitiable than frightening, though it was still frightening.

Reviews were, on the whole, scathing. One British critic suggested a "new rating: SO—Sadists Only!" But the box-office results amazed everyone involved. It wasn't merely a success. It was a *gigantic* success on both sides of the Atlantic. It became the most financially successful British film in years.

The die was cast. Frankenstein was back, and Hammer had him. Hammer made the two obvious follow-up choices: a Frankenstein sequel and a new version of Dracula. Both were even better, and both make our top-ten list. But first . . .

7. Curse of the Demon *(Columbia, 1957)*

"You said, 'Do your worst,' and that's precisely what I did."

Montague Rhodes James, usually billed as M.R. James, is one of the great masters of the English ghost story, and you can have a wonderfully spooky evening for yourself by snuggling down with a volume of his short stories. Ironically, his best-known tale, *Casting the Runes,* contains no ghosts at all, but rather is a narrative of demonology, black magic, and witchcraft. One of the very few of his tales to have been filmed, it is the basis of the most excellent British thriller released in America as *Curse of the Demon* and in England as *Night of the Demon.*

The Story: In 1957, American professional skeptic Dr. John Holden (Dana Andrews) travels to London to investigate a notorious English satanist and warlock,

Dr. Julian Karswell (Niall MacGinnis), leader of a black magic cult. His collaborator on the project, Dr. Harrington (Maurice Denham), has died under mysterious circumstances, shredded by a gigantic fire demon (himself).

Karswell invites Holden to his country estate, Lufford Hall, to examine a rare book of witchcraft missing from the British Museum's collection. Holden takes along Joanna Carrington (Peggy Cummins), his colleague's niece. They find Karswell engaged in the least sinister pastime imaginable, dressed as a tramp clown, entertaining children at a Halloween party, performing simple magic tricks. They also meet his dotty mother (Athene Seyler).

Karswell warns Holden off from investigating him. To give weight to his warning, he gives a small demonstration of his power. With just a moment's concentration, he conjures up a powerful windstorm that blows the party away. Karswell tells Holden he will die in three days.

Holden's colleagues have a man, Rand Hobart, in the hospital, catatonic since seeing, well, maybe a demon. It is proposed that they hypnotize Hobart to try and unlock his memories of whatever traumatized him.

Holden discovers that Karswell has slipped him a parchment with runes written on them. They learn that this is a spell. The holder of the parchment will be attacked by a demon unless he can pass the parchment back to the one who gave it to him.

The hypnotic treatment of Rand Hobart does not go well. Once hypnotized, Holden shows him the parchment. Hobart panics and jumps out a window to his death. At last, Holden is impressed. He decides that perhaps he should return the parchment to Karswell. He catches the South Hampton Train at Clapham Junction, knowing Karswell will be aboard. Karswell is now frightened that Holden will pass him back the parchment. Karswell dodges everything Holden tries to give him, a written retraction, a cigarette, even matches, but he slips up and takes his coat from Holden, who has slipped the parchment into his coat pocket.

The parchment flies out of Karswell's hand as he disembarks. As he chases it down the tracks, a demon the size of the Smithsonian Institution shows up and shreds him. When the police find his body, they think he was run over by a train. If only.

This scary and atmospheric thriller was directed by Jacques Tourneur, who also directed *Cat People* and *I Walked With a Zombie,* and it is the scariest movie Val Lewton never lived to make. Everything suggests a Lewton movie: the brilliant black-and-white photography, the eerie lighting effects, the way sound and suggestion are used to create terror out of almost nothing, even the studio interference.

The worst thing about the movie is the monster. The demon is gigantic but chintzy, and dopey looking. Its two appearances, at the top of the film and, even worse, at the end, ruin what is otherwise an intelligent and creepy picture. The shots were inserted by the producer, Hal Chester, over everyone else's objections.

The screenwriter, Charles Bennett, who had written many of Hitchcock's early successes, such as the first

Man Who Knew Too Much and *The 39 Steps,* was so angered by the intrusion of the fake-looking demon that he asked to have his name taken off the credits. Instead, Chester added his own name to the writing credits.

Niall MacGinnis steals the picture as Karswell. Most of the time he is remarkably affable, even charming. He plays against the menace for most of the film, so his few moments of showing authority in his threats carry more weight. He is given rich dialogue by Bennett to deliver, and wraps his golden voice around the lines, underplaying them with tremendous restraint. And he keeps the fear alive underneath his performance, so you always realize that he is as afraid as everyone else, a man not really in control of the massive evil forces he has foolishly called into being.

Athene Seyler, as his dotty, loveable mother, is also a scene-stealer, comic most of the time, yet despairing at the last. Peggy Cummins and Dana Andrews, though less effective, are solid, and their tiny romance never intrudes or derails the picture. The film, though updating James's tale to the then-present, and elaborating it for feature length, is otherwise quite faithful to the excellent original short story.

Shot at the same time as *Curse of Frankenstein,* it did not reach America until a year after it. In fact, it was released stateside in a butchered version (the DVD restores the film to its original version) as the lower half of a double bill with Hammer's first sequel, *The Revenge of Frankenstein,* which we will treat shortly, a powerhouse double bill if ever there was one.

8. Horror of Dracula *(Hammer, 1958)*

"We have it within our power to rid the world of this evil, and with God's help, we'll succeed."

Horror of Dracula and *Curse of Frankenstein* were re-released in America as a double bill in 1964. I'd been waiting to see them for several years. *Horror of Dracula* was on first. When it was over, I phoned my parents and asked them to pick me up at the theater 90 minutes later than planned, because I *had* to watch this movie a second time. Once through simply wasn't enough.

The Story: Jonathon Harker (John Van Eyssen) arrives at Castle Dracula. Dracula (Christopher Lee) has hired him as a librarian (huh?), but Harker is secretly a professional vampire fighter, there to kill the king of vampires. However, a female vampire (Valerie Gaunt) seduces Harker and bites him. Dracula bursts in, and has a fierce battle with the female vampire. Harker wakes up late the next day, and sees the bite on his throat. He finds the crypt where Dracula and his bride rest in their coffins. Harker stakes the female, but takes too long. The sun has set. Dracula has awoken.

Harker's associate, Dr. Van Helsing (Peter Cushing), arrives at Castle Dracula a few days later. Dracula is gone, but Harker, now a vampire, remains behind, and Van Helsing must put him to rest.

Van Helsing visits the family of Harker's fiancée, Lucy (Carol Marsh), where her brother, Arthur Holmwood (Michael Gough), is suspicious of Van Helsing. Lucy is not well, for Dracula is visiting her late each evening, in revenge for Harker's staking of his bride. Holmwood's wife, Mina (Melissa Stribling), asks Van

Helsing to give a second opinion about Lucy's anemia. Van Helsing instantly recognizes the symptoms of vampire-victimhood, and prescribes that bushels of garlic be placed all over the room and the French windows be kept closed at night. Lucy begs the maid to remove the garlic and open the windows, and the maid, taking her own medical opinion over that of *Dr.* Van Helsing, removes the garlic and opens the window. In the morning, Lucy is found dead.

Van Helsing leaves Harker's diary with Holmwood, so he can understand what happened to his sister. Meanwhile a policeman brings home the maid's little daughter, who tells of being tempted in the night by Lucy. Holmwood visits Lucy's tomb, but finds her coffin empty. Lucy enters with the child, but tries instead to bite her brother. She is fended off by Van Helsing with a crucifix. When he touches the crucifix to her forehead, it brands itself into her. Once back in her coffin, Van Helsing pounds a stake into her, as she shrieks.

As Van Helsing and Holmwood team up to track Dracula's movements, Dracula begins visiting Mina. When Holmwood hands her a crucifix to wear in his absence, it burns itself into her palm, and they realize their enemy is ahead of them. Van Helsing finds Dracula's coffin in the Holmwood wine cellar. Dracula grabs Mina, steals a coach, and heads for home. Van Helsing and Holmwood chase Dracula back to his castle, where they are just in time to prevent the count from burying Mina alive. Van Helsing rips down the curtains, flooding the room with the newly risen sun's light, which rots Dracula away to dust.

After the surprise runaway success of *Curse of*

Frankenstein, the logical follow-up was to tackle *Dracula* in the new style they had just created. The same team was reassembled: Terence Fisher again directing, and assuming the mantle of new master of gothic horror; Cushing and Lee reteamed, with Lee finding true stardom in what instantly became his trademark role, wiping Lugosi right off the screen; Jimmy Sangster again giving a very original twist to his adaptation of an often-told tale; Bernard Robinson again supplying a pulse-pounding, memorable musical score; and especially the gorgeous photography of Jack Asher. For years it seemed these stories belonged in black-and-white, but Asher's unique style of painting with light showed that gothic cinema was at home in Technicolor. Every frame of this movie is beautiful to look at, even the gore. It looks like a much more expensive picture than it is.

The impact of the explosions of violence were groundbreaking, and woke up audiences expecting a languid, Lugosi-type, talky vampire. Nothing like it had ever been seen before. Even its predecessor, *Curse of Frankenstein,* paled beside it.

Admittedly, it's probably the least-faithful-to-the-letter adaptation of Stoker's *Dracula* novel ever, but it captured the spirit and the impact of the book like nothing before or since. Lee's Count Dracula is jarring at first. He seems too young, and he sounds like he's spent more time in Oxford than Transylvania. But after ten minutes, Lee has no more dialogue in the whole movie. Like Dracula in the book, he lurks in the background of the story, periodically erupting into the foreground with a terrifying, wordless ferocity.

Fisher uses the camera like no one had before. Rather

than a lot of intercutting, he favors long takes with a moving camera that catches different set-ups, and allows his superb cast to establish their own acting rhythms. The picture is extremely well-paced, and rockets along without a dull moment.

Cushing's Van Helsing owes a lot to his Baron Frankenstein, but where Frankenstein is cold, ruthless, and superior, Van Helsing is compassionate, kind, and yet an articulate and determined man of action. And his precise delivery of the literate dialogue Sangster has provided is a treat for the ear.

As for Lee, there's no question about what he has brought new to the role: ferocity and sex. Lucy's eyes light up waiting for her forbidden midnight lover. Lee brought the sinister sex that always lay under Stoker's pages right onto the screen.

Fisher's camera suggests Dracula's approach with swirling leaves on Lucy's verandah. Fisher is often accused of ham-fisted sledgehammer tactics, but his subtlety apparently was too subtle for his critics.

There's a running theme in all of Fisher's gothics, a class-warfare hatred of the aristocracy. In Fisher's movies, evil always comes from aristocrats victimizing the under class. In his Frankenstein series (Fisher directed five of the six films in the series), it is the baron who is the continuing character, and he regards all lesser people (which is everyone) as test subjects and raw material. In the *Dracula* films, the evil count lives on for centuries by feeding on the blood of the peasants. In Fisher's 1960 *Curse of the Werewolf,* it is the cruelty and sadism of an old, diseased baron that spawns the lycanthropic curse.

Horror of Dracula, simply titled *Dracula* in England, was an even bigger hit than *Curse of Frankenstein.* The die was cast, and Hammer was to continue churning out gothic monster movies, of steadily decreasing quality, for another sixteen years.

9. The Revenge of Frankenstein (*Hammer, 1958*)

"I swore I would have my revenge. They will never get rid of me."

The Frankenstein Monster not only died at the end of *Curse of Frankenstein,* but his body was utterly destroyed in a vat of acid. It would not be coming back for a sequel. A very different approach from that of *Bride of Frankenstein* would be needed for Hammer's *Frankenstein* sequel.

The Story: *The Revenge of Frankenstein* begins with a shot of the same guillotine that *Curse* ended with. Baron Frankenstein (Peter Cushing) is led to the scaffold with the unsympathetic priest who has just listened to his story, and a misshapen jailer, Karl (Oscar Quitak). The blade rises, and then falls.

A pair of comic grave robbers (Lionel Jeffries and Michael Ripper) dig up the coffin of Baron Frankenstein, only to discover it contains the body of a headless priest. The alive-and-well Baron Frankenstein steps out of the shadows. One of the grave robbers runs off, while the other dies of fright, falling neatly into the freshly redug grave.

Three years later, in Carlsbruck, the local medical board is insulted that the superior Dr. Stein refuses to join their board. They send a delegation to confront him at his medical clinic for the poor, where Dr. Stein, assisted by Karl, gleefully insults them. One of them, Hans (Francis Matthews), remains behind. He has recognized Stein as Baron Frankenstein, and blackmails him into letting him become his apprentice, to learn from his genius.

Frankenstein shows Hans his secret lab, where he has been constructing a fresh body (Michael Gwynn) out of bits and pieces he amputates from his indigent patients at the clinic. He intends to transplant Karl's brain into this untwisted body, as repayment for saving him from execution. He has already transplanted the brain of an orangutan into a chimpanzee, giving new hope to sick orangutans everywhere.

A naive young girl named Margaret (Eunice Gayson) comes to volunteer at the clinic, and Karl forms an attachment to her. His operation goes well, but while the new Karl is recuperating, Hans stupidly tells him of the baron's plan to exhibit him to scientific scrutiny, which just means further freakdom to Karl. Margaret sneaks in to treat the mysterious new patient, and blunderingly allows him to escape. Meanwhile, the chimp with the brain of an orangutan turns carnivorous. The baron shows Hans the new body he has built, an exact duplicate of himself. (One wonders where he got the head.)

Karl returns to the lab and destroys the remains of his old body. He is caught by a brutal landlord, who beats him savagely, which awakens Karl's bloodlust. Karl kills the landlord, and finds that his new body is starting to twist like his old one. He hides in Margaret's barn, and later attacks and kills a girl in a park, perhaps even eating a bit of her.

Karl crashes a society ball at Margaret's home, and begs Frankenstein to help him, and then keels over dead, in front of everybody. Word spreads all over Carlsbruck that Dr. Stein is Baron Frankenstein. The patients at the clinic, realizing they have been used as an organ-and-limb farm, attack the baron and beat him almost to death. Hans transplants the dying baron's brain into the new body.

A few years later, in London, Dr. Franck opens his clinic. It is, of course, Baron Frankenstein in his new body. The baron and his monster have fused, become one, and he's back to his old, bad habits.

Generally considered an improvement on the first Hammer Frankenstein, it is surer and brisker, although Michael Gwynn doesn't make much of a monster. It certainly has roamed far afield from Mary Shelley's book. Cushing is thoroughly at home now in the role, and enjoys the sarcasm the baron is given to dispensing. The photography of Jack Asher continues to bring beauty to gruesome images. Eunice Gayson, who plays the simpering heroine, also holds the distinction of being the first Bond girl, Sylvia Trench, the woman who, in the opening scenes of *Dr. No,* asks Sean Connery his name at the gaming table, giving him the straight line for his first-ever announcement of "Bond, James Bond," and then shows up at Bond's apartment to distract him with some half-nude golf.

The film led to four more sequels: *The Evil of Frankenstein* (1963), *Frankenstein Created Woman* (1967), *Frankenstein Must Be Destroyed* (1969), and *Frankenstein and the Monster From Hell* (1973), all but *Evil* directed by Fisher, and all starring Peter Cushing. If none is as good as *Bride of Frankenstein* or *Son of Frankenstein,* all are *vastly* better than *Frankenstein Meets the Wolfman.*

10. The Mummy *(Hammer, 1959)*

"It seems the best part of my life has been spent among the dead."

Universal could hardly fail to note Hammer's ongoing success in the late 1950s, recycling the same monsters it had monopolized for so long. Deciding to cash in, particularly since all the risk was Hammer's, it entered into an American distribution deal with Hammer, and offered up the rights to its own monsters. The novels *Frankenstein* and *Dracula* were in the public domain, so anyone could shoot movies with those stories and characters, as long as they didn't traipse onto Universal's trademarked make-ups, which is why Lee's Frankenstein Monster looks nothing like Karloff's. But now Hammer could remake *The Mummy.*

The Story: In 1895, a British archeological expedition, led by Stephen Banning (Felix Aylmer) and Joseph Whemple (Raymond Huntley), finds and opens the tomb of the Princess Ananka, ignoring the warning of the Egyptian zealot Mehemet (George Pastell) that "he who robs the tombs of Egypt dies." Banning's son John (Peter Cushing) can not join them in the tomb, as he has broken his leg. Something causes Stephen Banning, when left alone in the tomb, to go insane.

Back in England, three years later, John Banning and his French wife, Isobel (Yvonne Furneaux), are summoned to the insane asylum where Banning's father lives. Stephen Banning has regained some lucidity, and warns his son that there was a second mummy in the tomb, and a scroll of life that can awaken it. The Mummy, he says, hates them for desecrating the tomb of Ananka, and will kill them all. John merely assumes his father is still raving.

Mehemet has, in fact, re-excavated the tomb, and recovered the mummy of Kharis (Christopher Lee) and the scroll, which were hidden in a secret room. Now Mehemet has taken up residence near the Bannings, and is having the Mummy shipped to him. The drunken cart drivers lose the crate containing the Mummy when it falls off the cart and sinks into a muddy bog. Mehemet reads the scroll of life over the bog, which resurrects Kharis, who clambers out of the swamp. Mehemet sends him out to kill the unbelievers who defiled Ananka's tomb. Kharis marches off, breaks into the asylum, and kills Banning.

John tells Whemple the tale of Kharis and Ananka, of how in 2,000 BC, the Princess Ananka died of an illness while on a pilgrimage. Many members of the funeral procession were sacrificed at her entombment. After all the funeral rites, Kharis returned to the tomb in secret with the scroll of life. Kharis was Ananka's secret, blasphemous lover. He attempted to raise her mummy to life, but he was caught before he could complete the profane ceremony. Kharis's tongue was cut out, and he was entombed alive, to guard the princess for all time. The scroll was also entombed in a gimmicked container that, if pulled out, will open the secret panel that releases Kharis. Whemple pooh-poohs the whole story as "historical myth."

Mehemet sends Kharis out again, and John sees it

kill Whemple, and shoots it repeatedly. The police find Banning's story hard to swallow. Banning tells the police inspector that he believes that when his father was alone in Ananka's tomb, he found the scroll of life, foolishly read it aloud, releasing and reviving Kharis. The sight of the living mummy was what sent Stephen mad. Only the arrival of Mehemet had kept Kharis from killing Stephen then. The police inspector doesn't buy any of it.

Banning finally notices that his wife is a dead ringer for Ananka. When the Mummy shows up to kill John, he is saved by his wife's pretending to be Ananka, and ordering Kharis off.

This time the inspector starts to believe the story. He tells Banning about the Egyptian man who has moved in nearby. Banning goes to see Mehemet. The conversation begins politely, but turns nasty. Mehemet points up the immorality of robbing the dead, while Banning deliberately answers him dismissively and rudely, referring to Karnak as a "third-rate god," and accusing his believers of having a "standard of intelligence that must be remarkably low." He is clearly baiting Mehemet. It works.

Mehemet accompanies Kharis when he sends him after Banning once again. Again it is Isobel's impersonation of Ananka that stops Kharis from strangling Banning. When Mehemet orders Kharis to kill Isobel, he makes a fatal mistake. Kharis breaks Mehemet's back, and then carries Isobel off to the bog. Isobel manages to get Kharis to let her go. Once she's clear of him, the police shoot him full of holes, and Kharis sinks at last to his rest in the bog.

Hammer's *The Mummy* is an odd mix. It takes the characters of the Bannings and Joseph Whemple from *The Mummy* with Boris Karloff, but Kharis, Ananka, and most of the plot come from Universal's Kharis movies, albeit making a film from it vastly superior to the whole Universal series. It should be noted that while Isobel looks exactly like Ananka, the film never states or implies that she is a reincarnation of the princess.

Prior to this movie, only Creighton Chaney had played Frankenstein's Monster, Dracula, and Kharis, the Mummy, but Lee now had also played all three roles, and far better than Chaney. His Kharis, a mute role except for the extended flashback to ancient Egypt, is not merely a robotic mummy slouching about. His pain and heartbreak show in his eyes, and in his walk, and in the way he uses his body. Lee takes what seems a thankless role, and brings unique qualities to it.

Cushing, stuck with a limp throughout the picture, makes another fascinating portrait. His John Banning is sympathetic, but also callous and a tad intolerant. One can see from the family dynamic with his bilious, self-involved father how he acquired his more negative qualities, and the limp remains a visual reminder of how his upbringing has emotionally crippled him.

Beautiful Yvonne Furneaux's next film was Fellini's *La Dolce Vita*. In an interview she recounted how, when Fellini learned her previous film was a Hammer horror, she could see his opinion of her nose-dive.

The film is gorgeously mounted, especially all the Egyptian trappings for the Ananka funeral scenes, which are remarkably extensive. Frank Reizenstein contributed a particularly beautiful music score. Sadly, this was Jack Asher's last time shooting a Terence Fisher Hammer horror movie. His images are just as painterly and sumptuous as ever, but the Hammer brass, ever cost-conscious, grew impatient with the time it took Asher to achieve his look, and he was never rehired. Although the Hammer films of the sixties continued to look handsome, Asher's unique use of colored light was never equaled by the subsequent cinematographers who worked there.

Kharis did find his rest, however. Although Hammer made a couple more mummy films, none of them was truly a sequel—they featured other mummies—and none came near the beauty and creepy terror of this great mummy classic.

The Honorable Mentions

Invaders From Mars *(National Pictures Corporation, 1953)*

Originally released in 3-D, and directed by William Cameron Menzies, the production designer of *Gone With the Wind*, this low-budget cheapie featuring laughable Martian monsters with visible zippers up the back, was a genuine nightmare for kids of the 1950s. A small boy (Jimmy Hunt) sees a flying saucer land in the sand pit behind his suburban home. Dad (Leif Ericson) goes to check it out, and comes back as *one of them!* When he tries to tell the police, Mom (Hilary Brooke) comes to pick him up, and she is now *one of them!* His little playmate next door is *one of them!* Could anything be more frightening to a child than to find that Mom and Dad have become alien monsters bent on his destruction? And if all that wasn't bad enough, at the end, he wakes up and finds it was all a dream. Whew! Only then, he sees the ship landing through the window and realizes, *This time it's for real!* For anyone under teen age, this was perhaps the scariest movie of the decade.

Godzilla, King of the Monsters
(Toho Productions, 1954)

Made in Japan as *Gojira,* where it was, inexplicably, a respected movie, the American distributor recut it, shaved off a lot of footage, and shot new footage with Raymond Burr as Steve Martin, which two decades later became an unfortunate name choice. The filmmakers were honest about it being "inspired" by Harryhausen's technically superior *Beast From 20,000 Fathoms,* but instead of Harryhausen's painstaking stop-motion animation, this has quintessential man-in-a-rubber-dinosaur-suit special effects. Further, Godzilla is about 400 times larger than any dinosaur known to have lived, and breathes radioactive fire. He's really a gigantic dragon. But while Harryhausen's *Beast* is a movie about atomic-bomb anxieties made by the country that dropped the bomb on cities full of people, and seems to float guilt-free, with the army coming to the rescue, *Godzilla* is a movie about atomic-bomb anxieties made by the people we dropped the bomb on, and it's a more serious, somber film, from people who knew what the experience was really like. The scientist who saves the world from Godzilla dies with it, to keep his evil discovery from wreaking more damage. It has a morose but memorable musical score. The original Japanese version is now available on DVD, and it is better than the Burr version, but not by much. It has inspired dozens of sequels, and a dreadful American remake shaming the résumé of Matthew Broderick.

THEM! *(Warner Bros., 1954)*

Another of the giant-monster, atomic-bomb-anxiety movies. This time it's ants exposed to the atomic tests of the 1940s, which have mutated into a species the size of suburban houses. They take up residence in the sewers under the streets of Los Angeles. Scientist Edmund Gwenn and cops James Whitmore and James Arness (now granted a human, speaking role after his turn as the Thing) save the world from the overgrown insects. This movie, which has a fairly intelligent script, featured full-sized, mechanical giant ants that look like crude Disneyland ride exhibits. Godzilla has better-looking special effects. Inexplicably, this picture was nominated for a special-effects Oscar. Wisely, it lost.

It Came From Beneath the Sea *(Columbia, 1955)*

Still another giant-monster, atomic-bomb-anxiety movie. This time, a giant octopus ravages San Francisco, and rips down part of the Golden Gate Bridge until Kenneth Tobey kills it. Ray Harryhausen's beautiful animation lifts the movie above its dopey script. To save money on the animation, the giant cephalopod has only six tentacles, so it's really a hexopus or, even better, a sexopus. The script undermines its own nascent feminism. Chauvinist Tobey tries to send female scientist Faith Domergue away from danger. There's a speech about how women are now the equals of men, and Faith says, "Besides, you underestimate my ability to help in a crisis." Two seconds later, a giant tentacle rises from the sea, and Faith screams her lungs out. Score one for male chauvinism. San Francisco refused to allow shooting on the Golden Gate Bridge because the movie would "undermine public confidence in the bridge." They apparently thought people wouldn't use the bridge because of their terror that *a giant octopus might tear it down!* The movie has been out now for fifty-two years, and public confidence in the bridge remains high, as does public contempt for the stupidity of public officials.

The Creeping Unknown *(Hammer, 1955)*

Known in England as *The Quatermass Xperiment*—the misspelling of *experiment* emphasizing the British *X* was a certificate issued to movies deemed too scary for kids—this was a black-and-white adaptation of a very intelligent television serial, the first of four built around rocket scientist Bernard Quatermass, all eventually filmed. This intelligent and scary film tells of the first astronaut (from the *British* space program—yeah, it was the English who landed on the moon first) who returns to earth infected with an alien organism that causes him to slowly mutate into a giant monster holed up in Westminster Abbey. Richard Wordsworth's performance as the tortured astronaut changing into a monster gives this film it's unforgettably haunting quality, and makes the waste of Wordsworth in small, thankless roles in future Hammer horrors inexplicable. This film helped steer Hammer in the direction of gothic monsters.

I Was a Teenage Werewolf *(AIP, 1957)*

It sounds silly, but is it? Yes. Very silly. Michael Landon is a bitter, hostile teenage rebel. Whit Bissell is the sinister scientist who hypnotizes him to unleash his inner beast, and turns him into a hairy-faced kid in a varsity jacket, slavering over sexy co-eds before eating them. Shot on a shoestring budget, and aimed cynically at the youth market, it was a huge hit, and led directly to . . .

I Was a Teenage Frankenstein *(AIP, 1957)*

Whit Bissell is the Frankenstein descendant making a hunky teenager out of spare parts gathered from hot-rod accident victims. Leftover raw materials he feeds to his crocodiles kept in a pit below the lab. The Monster (Gary Conway) has a face of grotesque putty, but from the neck down, he is pure muscle hunk in a tight T-shirt. Only in the last scene does he finally get Conway's pretty face. (Conway later was the first-ever *Playgirl* nude centerfold.) When the Monster tosses his mad creator into his machinery in a shower of sparks, it switches to color for the last few seconds. Idiotic, but it was another big hit.

20,000 Miles to Earth *(Columbia, 1957)*

A spaceship sent from earth to Venus, (Venus? The temperature on Venus is 900 degrees—I hope that ship was air-conditioned), returns and crashes into the Mediterranean Sea just off the coast of Sicily. Before it sinks, local fishermen rescue the surviving astronaut (William Hopper), and the egg of a Ymir, a Venusian creature that lives on sulfur. Once it hatches, it grows like crazy, and eventually goes on a rampage in Rome until shot down near the ancient Coliseum. The annoying little boy featured in the picture was played by Bart Braverman, as "Bart Bradley," later to become famous on the TV series *Vegas*. Not exactly sophisticated (a town full of poor Sicilian fishermen all speak English), the picture is elevated by the sympathy engendered for the Monster, born on the wrong planet, and by Ray Harryhausen's sparkling animation. Fun fact: the picture was set in Italy because Ray was bored with life in Los Angeles, and wanted to be paid to visit Italy.

The Blob *(Tonylyn Productions, 1958)*

Famed as the screen debut of Steve McQueen, this silly, inept, extremely low-budget color movie features the most basic, elemental, simple monster of all time, a blob of protoplasmic space ooze that eats any living thing it encounters, can't be killed, and just keeps growing. The good guys are all teenagers to attract the youth market, which it most successfully did. It's silly, but it works, and is quite entertaining. Eventually the blob is frozen and then dropped onto the Arctic ice cap, to stay frozen forever, so *beware of global warming!* It could unleash the Blob! There was an overtly comic sequel titled *Son of Blob* directed by Larry Hagman. When I mentioned to Larry Hagman last year that I had paid money to see *Son of Blob,* he replied, "You want your money back? Because I'll write you a check right now." Actually, I enjoyed it.

The Hound of the Baskervilles *(Hammer, 1958)*

Sir Arthur Conan Doyle's most famous Sherlock Holmes mystery is a ghost story where it all turns out to be a murder plot by a bad guy. Every film version of it (and there are dozens) is scary to some degree, but only Hammer's 1958 version went all out for horror, putting its horror A-team—Terence Fisher, Peter Cushing, Christopher Lee, and Jack Asher—on the project. The film is probably the least-faithful-to-the-novel version, with a black-magic, human-sacrifice angle added to the story, a scary exploration of unstable mines sequence, and Stapleton's virtuous wife changed to a bitter, vicious Spanish daughter (played by an Italian actress, Marla Landi, with an accent so thick she's unintelligible, and more spitefully hateful than the primary villain.) Still, it's an entertaining and scary movie. Peter Cushing makes a superb Sherlock Holmes, and went on to play the role many more times. Lee makes an unsympathetic Sir Henry Baskerville, but he has a fun moment when an ad-lib by Miles Malleson makes him smirk out of character in one shot. The biggest problem is that the monster when we finally get to it, the Hell Hound, was played by a big, friendly doggie that had spent too much time on the set getting to love the cast. When it has to attack Stapleton, you can see the actor grab the dog and pull it onto himself. The "evil beast" clearly just wants to romp and play. It becomes more like *The Big, Friendly Pooch of the Baskervilles*. In his lovely memoir, *Past Forgetting,* Peter Cushing tells of their trying to make the doggie look more formidable by dressing up young boys in his, Lee's and André Morell's (Dr. Watson) costumes, and shooting long shots of them chased by the beast. Cushing wrote of viewing the rushes: "We saw three small boys dressed up as if playing a game of

Q FACTS: The Gruesome Horseshoe!

The dance-hall set used for the can-can scene in *House of Wax* will look familiar to anyone who ever enjoyed *The Golden Horseshoe Review* at Disneyland. The set was designed by genius production designer Harper Goff for the Doris Day western musical, *Calamity Jane.* Shortly after that film, Goff left Warner Bros. for Walt Disney Studios, where he designed Disney's memorable *20,000 Leagues Under the Sea,* as well as a lot of Disneyland, then under construction. When Walt asked Harper to design his Frontierland saloon, the Golden Horseshoe, Harper just handed him the blueprints for the *Calamity Jane/House of Wax* dance-hall set, and picked up a second check. I told you he was a *genius!* Therefore, the Golden Horseshoe Saloon is identical, down to the smallest detail, to the set seen in the Vincent Price shocker, which may have creeped out more than a few movie fans as they enjoyed the antics of comic Wally Boag in *The Golden Horseshoe Review,* the show Boag co-wrote and co-starred in for over *40,000* performances. Singing the same songs and telling the same jokes over 40,000 times? Now *that* is true horror!

THAT DAMN BUTTON

In *Forbidden Planet* we progress from the lever that will blow up the lab in *Bride of Frankenstein* to a button that, once pushed, starts a chain-reaction "that can not be reversed," and blows up the whole planet. This seems like a very bad idea to me. One crazy Krell terrorist would be all it would take. *Why* do movie mad-scientists keep making these buttons and levers? Let's hope there isn't one for earth.

charades, foggy toy scenery with a wet, hungry dog in the middle, contentedly wolfing a bone. The sequence was scrapped."

House on Haunted Hill
(Allied Artists, 1959)

This one is a William Castle gimmick production, which presents a haunted house that isn't really haunted at all. Vincent Price hosts a "murder party" for a group of strangers in a supposedly haunted house. All the spooks and scares turn out to be part of an idiotically overcomplicated plot by Price to murder his unbearable wife. The exteriors are of a gorgeous Frank Lloyd Wright house in Hollywood. The interiors are in another architectural style altogether, that of no-budget sets. The gimmick this time was "Emergo": When a character is menaced by a walking skeleton, a skeleton on a wire sailed out over the heads of the audience. Price's acting

DUEL OF THE DRACULAS

In Hammer's 1959 *The Mummy,* Raymond Huntley plays the small role of Joseph Whemple. Huntley was the *original* Count Dracula on the London stage, and toured in the role for decades. It was the play he had scored in that Lugosi did on Broadway—and only because Huntley was too busy doing the role all over Great Britain. Having him in a film with Christopher Lee was a meeting of two great Draculas. And given how Huntley's Dracula is now forgotten, while Lee's lives on, it seems only appropriate that Lee kills Huntley in the film.

is much better than the movie around it, and helped position him for his ascension to a horror throne in 1960.

The Tingler *(Allied Artists, 1959)*

Another William Castle–Vincent Price gimmick movie. This one has a really insane premise. When we're frightened, the movie says, a creature called a tingler grows on our spine and will kill us unless we scream, which makes it shrivel up and go away. Okay. When a mute woman is terrified by her sadistic husband, her inability to scream allows her tingler to kill her. The thing escapes during her autopsy and runs around tingling people to death until finally vanquished by heroic Vincent Price. For this gimmick, "Percepto," the creature gets loose in a movie theater. Price warns the movie audience to scream for their lives. Theater seats were wired up to vibrate at this moment, causing easily scared teenagers to shriek. The tingler is even sillier than the Blob. Romantic leads Darryl Hickman and Patricia Cutts met making this film. They married soon after, and are still married today. *Aaahh.*

QUOTE

Peter was the great perfectionist, who learned not only his own lines, but everybody else's as well. But withal had a gentle humor which made it quite impossible for anybody to be pompous in his company."—*Christopher Lee.*

He is a man of many attributes, among them a most marvelous sense of humor, plus the ability to laugh at himself."—*Peter Cushing*

There have been great comedy teams: Laurel and Hardy, Abbott and Costello, Rowan and Martin, the Marx Brothers. Romantic or musical teams: Gable and Lombard, MacDonald and Eddy, Astaire and Rogers. But horror teams? Karloff and Lugosi made eight films together; however, these were usually cynical attempts to force-create a horror team by the studios.

But Peter Cushing and Christopher Lee made twenty-two films together, and I will argue that we could actually raise that count to twenty-four. *Psycho* author Robert Bloch, who wrote two of the Cushing and Lee films, called them "the Gruesome Twosome," and he meant it with the same kind of overwhelming affection that every one of their acquaintances uses when speaking of them. If ever there was a true horror team, then Cushing and Lee is it.

Peter Wilton Cushing was born on May 26, 1913, in Surrey, England. Cushing's mother, already having a son, wanted a girl this time around, so for the first two years of his life, Peter was the world's youngest transvestite, clothed in dresses and ribbons, with long curly hair, until his embarrassed father finally put a halt to it.

Although Cushing's father was a surveyor, there was theater in Peter's blood. His aunt was Lillie Langtry's understudy. His Uncle Wilton, for whom he was given his middle name, was an actor and playwright, and his grandfather was a member of Sir Henry Irving's acting company, managed by Bram Stoker, the author of *Dracula*. Now there's a coincidence that is truly *spooky!*

Cushing's father was fiercely opposed to Peter's theatrical ambitions, and insisted on sticking him at a desk in the county surveyor's office. Cushing was miserable, and continued to study acting and practice diction relentlessly, achieving the marvelous, precise speech we know from his films. Eventually he was able to enter repertory companies, and leave the office behind forever.

In 1939, he made the bold step of moving to Hollywood, where he was given his first movie job by the great master of the gothic cinema himself, James Whale. In Whale's *The Man in the Iron Mask,* Louis Hayward played identical twins. For the effects scenes where Hayward had to act opposite himself, Cushing played opposite him. Hayward would play the twin on the right, and Cushing the twin on the left. They'd shoot it. Then they'd reverse, and Hayward played the twin on the left, Cushing the one on the right. In editing, Cushing was trimmed out, and Hayward laid in. It was the star role, only he was never seen, except for a brief bit as a messenger, given him by Whale so he could have at least a moment or two onscreen.

Hayward and his wife, Ida Lupino, were so taken by Cushing that they allowed the struggling actor to live in their home for his two years in California.

Cushing's second film role was opposite Laurel and Hardy in their picture *A Chump at Oxford,* where he appears young and fresh-faced, as a bullying upperclassman hazing Stan and Ollie.

During this period, he also played cricket regularly with Boris Karloff and Basil Rathbone. Yes, two of the three great Sherlock Holmeses played cricket together, and Hammer's Baron Frankenstein hit the pitch each week with Universal's Frankenstein Monster. Cushing appeared in five more American films, including acting opposite Cary Grant in *The Howards of Virginia,* before the outbreak of World War II motivated him to return to England, though en route he found time to make his only Broadway appearance, for the eleven performances of the bomb *Seventh Trumpet.*

Torn knee ligaments kept him out of the army, but not out of ENSA (the Entertainment of the National Services Association), where he starred in Noel Coward's *Private Lives,* in which he met Russian-born Helen Beck, who in 1943 became Helen Cushing, the love of his life.

In 1948, Laurence Olivier cast Cushing as Osric, an effeminate, comic-relief fop, in his film of Shakespeare's *Hamlet.* Also in *Hamlet,* in a teeny part as a guard, allowed to say no more than "Lights! The king wants light," was a very tall young man named Christopher Lee. They had no scenes together, and did not meet at that time, but nonetheless, *Hamlet,* a story of a man driven to avenge family murder by a ghost—prime Hammer horror material—is the first Cushing and Lee film.

Olivier liked Cushing so much that he was invited to join's Olivier's Old Vic touring company on a tour of Australia. Olivier kept Cushing under contract and working through the early 1950s. One film he made in this period was John Huston's *Moulin Rouge* (1952). Also in the cast was Christopher Lee, so this is Cushing and Lee film number two, even though not only did they not meet, but Cushing's scenes were all shot in England, while Lee's scenes were shot in Paris.

Around this time, Cushing began appearing in TV dramas, and it was here that his star really began to rise. In particular, his performances as Mr. Darcy in a TV adaptation of *Pride and Prejudice,* and as Winston Smith in a TV adaptation of George Orwell's *1984,* made a household name of him in Great Britain. When Hammer was casting *Curse of Frankenstein* in 1957, Cushing was cast in large part because he was now a big TV star in England. The writing was on the wall, *in blood!*

Christopher Frank Carandini Lee was born May 27, 1922, in London, England. His father was Lieutenant Geoffrey Trollope Lee, and his mother was *Contessa* Estelle Maria Carandini. The Carandinis were one of Italy's six oldest families, with a lineage stretching back over 900 years. Recent archeological findings establish the Carandinis as a moneyed family all the way back to the time of Christ. Lt. Lee divorced his Italian countess when Christopher was six. He, his mother, and his older sister went to live in Switzerland. In school plays there at the age of six, he learned, as he later wrote in his fascinating autobiography *Lord of Misrule,* that "the best lines are given to the baddies, and that these make the most impact on the audience."

After a short period, the family returned to London, and his mother married a wealthy banker named Harcourt George St. Croix Rose, who was the uncle of a lad named Ian Fleming. Lee's new cousin would go on to create James Bond, and to eventually recommend his tall cousin for the title role in *Dr. No,* though Lee's Bond villain, Saramanga in *The Man With the Golden Gun,* wouldn't come about until after Fleming's death. One night, when still a small boy, he was awakened in order to meet Prince Yusupoff and the Grand Duke Dmitri, the men who assassinated Rasputin. One wonders if Lee, the future star of Hammer's *Rasputin, the Mad Monk,* felt an echo from his future fictional grave.

At prep school in Oxford, he acted several times with school chum Patrick MacNee, the future John Steed of

The Avengers, as well as a man destined to be Dr. Watson to Lee's Sherlock Holmes sixty years later.

Although he had acted almost from birth, it had not occurred to him to pursue acting professionally. However, during World War II, he took up the most deadly form of acting known to man. For British Intelligence, he became a genuine spy. As he wrote in his autobiography: "As the new spy, I found myself like an actor, taking on a part in a long-running play. Except that here, the actors were obliged for their lives to depend on me." For a year and a half after the war, he was involved in war-crimes investigations, during the course of which he met Joseph Stalin. Much of Lee's war exploits are still classified, and Lee refuses to discuss those. All we know for certain is that he was a genuine war hero, a real-life James Bond. I wonder how he kept a straight face on the set of *The Man with the Golden Gun,* watching Roger Moore, the lamest of all the Bonds, going though his pathetic paces.

It was the casual suggestion of an Italian cousin in 1946 that finally dropped the penny on Lee's career choice. Through family connections he became a contract player for the Rank Organization, although at first his great height—he is six foot four—was considered a drawback.

Lee is a man of learning and accomplishment. He speaks seven languages, and can read and write several more. He is an operatic bass and has sung in operas the world round. He reads voraciously, and cultivated many literary friends. When making the Peter Jackson movies of *The Lord of the Rings,* Lee was revered on the set as the only person, out of the hundreds employed on the movie, who had actually known and been a friend of J.R.R. Tolkien.

When Rank finally released him from his contract (for being too tall and not looking sufficiently English), he used his linguistic skills to work as an actor all over Europe. One notable early role was as the swashbuckling henchman to the villain opposite Burt Lancaster in *The Crimson Pirate* for Robert Siodmak, appropriately the director of *Son of Dracula*. On *The Warriors,* Lee almost lost a finger when Errol Flynn cut it half off in an accident shooting a broadsword duel. Determined to prove Rank wrong, Lee did TV, stage, movies, operas, and extensive voice-over work, often providing voices when dubbing foreign-language films into English, and English films into other languages. One of the films he dubbed into English was the Jacques Tati classic *Monsieur Hulot's Holiday.* In some films, Lee did *all* the voices, even the women's.

Eventually, as he knew it would, his liability became his saving grace, for it was his height that landed Lee the role as the Frankenstein Monster, and while it was not the star-making role it had been for Karloff, it led to his casting as Count Dracula, and that role *did* make him the star he remains to this day.

In his memoir, Lee has this to say of his first meeting with Cushing, on what was their third mutual film, *Curse of Frankenstein*: "Our very first encounter began with me storming into his dressing room and announcing in petulant tones, 'I haven't got any lines.' He looked up, his mouth twitched, and he said dryly, "You're lucky. I've read the script.'"

The chemistry between these two funny, intelligent

men was immediately apparent, and after *Horror of Dracula*, they were paired again eighteen more times, not always for Hammer: *The Hound of the Baskervilles* (1959), *The Mummy* (1959), *The Gorgon* (1964), *Dr. Terror's House of Horrors* (1965), *She* (1965), *The Skull* (1965), *Island of the Burning Damned* (1967), *Scream and Scream Again* (1970, also with Vincent Price), *One More Time* (1970), *The House That Dripped Blood* (1971), *I, Monster* (1972, with Lee as Jekyll and Hyde), *Dracula AD 1972* (1972), *Horror Express* (1972), *The Creeping Flesh* (1973), *Nothing but the Night* (1974), *The Satanic Rites of Dracula* (1974), *Arabian Adventure* (1979), and *House of the Long Shadows* (1983, also with Vincent Price).

Everyone, and I mean *everyone,* who knew Peter Cushing loved him. Everyone who worked with him respected him. Everyone who spent time with him adored his sense of humor. Of his film *Madhouse,* where he was teamed with Vincent Price, Price wrote in a magazine article: "Yesterday, Peter had to fall into a tank of spiders. It is very difficult to fall into a tank of spiders, and be Brando."

In 1971, Helen Cushing died after a long illness, and part of Peter died with her. He mourned the rest of his life, and he lived another twenty-three years. He never remarried, and some of the force went out of him, but he not only continued acting until 1983, but his greatest success, a little sci-fi space opera called *Star Wars,* came in 1977. Incidentally, Darth Vader, who plays most of his scenes with Cushing, was played by David Prowse. Four years earlier, Prowse had been Peter's last Frankenstein Monster in *Frankenstein and the Monster From Hell.*

Lee married Bridgit Kroencke, always know as Gitte, in 1961. They are still married today. They have one daughter, Christina, whose birthday, November 23, is also the birthday of Boris Karloff and *his* daughter, Sarah Jane. For that matter, Lee's birthday is the same as Vincent Price's, and Cushing's is the day before. Hmmm.

Lee relocated to California in the early seventies for ten years, determined to expand his career beyond gothics, though without ever really abandoning them altogether, where I was privileged to meet him several times. His insanely gigantic film résumé (larger than any other major star's) includes a series of films as Fu Manchu, an episode of *Alfred Hitchcock Presents*, *Curse of the Crimson Alter* (one of two films with his London next-door-neighbor, Boris Karloff), *The Oblong Box* (with Vincent Price), *De Sade, The Magic Christian, The Private Life of Sherlock Holmes, Julius Caesar, Hannie Caulder, The Wicker Man* (his favorite picture and role), *The Three Musketeers* and *The Four Musketeers, Airport '77, Return from Witch Mountain* (a Disney movie with Bette Davis), *1941, Gremlins 2: The New Batch*. He even hosted *Saturday Night Live*. Among the great directors he has worked with are Billy Wilder, Richard Lester, Joe Danté, Steven Spielberg, George Lucas, Tim Burton, and Peter Jackson.

Cushing and Lee worked together one last time, on May 19, 1994, when they recorded the narration for a documentary on the history of Hammer horror, in a studio in London. Peter Cushing died three months later, on August 11, 1994.

Today, in his eighties, Lee is bigger than ever. Over the last decade he has appeared in *Sleepy Hollow, The*

Corpse Bride, Charlie and the Chocolate Factory, two *Star Wars* movies, and all three *Lord of the Rings* pictures. That's eight blockbuster hits in a row. That's a better streak than Harrison Ford in the 1980s. And he shows no signs of retiring any time soon, or indeed ever.

Oh, and those two iffy Cushing and Lee titles? Well, in Stanley Kubrick's great black comedy *Lolita* (1962), there's a scene where James Mason, Shelley Winters, and Sue Lyon all go to a drive-in movie. The movie they are watching is *Curse of Frankenstein,* the scene where Lee's monster rips off his bandages and tries to throttle Cushing's Baron Frankenstein. They are both in *Lolita,* so I count it.

And the other? Well, in George Lucas's 2005 *Star Wars, Episode III, Revenge of the Sith,* Lee has a major scene early on as the villainous Count Dooku, a.k.a. Darth Sidious. At the end of the picture, when the fully reconstituted Darth Vader assumes his place on the ship's bridge, a character identified as "Governor Tarkin" in the credits, and who is a dead ringer for a young Peter Cushing, is seen taking an order and walking away.

Of course, all *Star Wars* fans know that Peter Cushing's *Star Wars* character is Grand Moff Tarkin, in a film taking place twenty years later. On the movie's DVD commentary track, effects animator Rob Coleman explains that at first he planned to recreate a digital Peter Cushing, and even discussed Cushing with Lee for this purpose. But they found an actor in Sydney, Australia, Wayne Pygram, who looked a lot like Cushing, and then made him up using prosthetic pieces cast from a life mask of Cushing, to duplicate his wonderful face. Thus, through the wonders of make-up technology and respectful filmmakers, *Star Wars, Episode III, Revenge of the Sith* became one last Cushing and Lee film, eleven years *after* Peter Cushing's death. Baron Frankenstein had been raised, however briefly, from the dead. When I spotted the ersatz Cushing while watching the movie in a theater in Hollywood, I teared up. It was a lovely last salute to a wonderful man and a wonderful team.

May the force be with them.

The Never-Ending Picture Show

The Legacy

> "Frankenstein make him live for *always!*"

WE'RE COMING TO A HALT HERE AT 1960. Thanks to the television release of the Universal pictures of the Golden and Silver Age monster movies, the success of the Hammer films, and the popularity of "Monster Magazines" led by Forest J. Ackerman's pioneering *Famous Monsters of Filmland,* Baby-Boomers had fallen in love with Karloff, Lugosi, Creighton Chaney, whom they knew only as Lon Jr., on TV, while Price, Cushing, and Lee were scaring and delighting them in theaters each week. Monsters had never been healthier, and the sixties would be a new Golden Age.

In 1960, two of the three highest-grossing films were horror movies. One of them, *The Fall of the House of Usher,* was the first of the Roger Corman–Vincent

Price–Edgar Allan Poe–American International Pictures widescreen color thrillers, and its huge success shortly transformed AIP into the American Hammer, with Price dominating its output, but with Boris Karloff, Peter Lorre, Basil Rathbone, and even Creighton Chaney brought back to end their days thrilling a new generation.

When Poe had been exhausted, the works of H.P. Lovecraft were plundered, and in a desperate pinch, original works were made. Often the name of Poe was attached to films to which his connection was tenuous, if not nonexistent. *Edgar Allan Poe's The Haunted Palace* was really a film of H.P. Lovecraft's novel *The Case of Charles Dexter Ward*. A British AIP film with Vincent Price about the historical figure Matthew Hopkins, titled *Witchfinder General,* was released in America as *Edgar Allen Poe's The Conqueror Worm.* Poe's actual relationship to the movie was that they stuck his name in the title. For that matter, Roger Corman's *The Raven,* with Price, Karloff, Lorre, Hazel Court, and Jack Nicholson, is a ninety-minute comedy about dueling thirteenth-century wizards based on Poe's two-page poem about a bereaved man expressing his grief and depression over a lover's recent death.

The other big 1960 horror success was Alfred Hitchcock's *Psycho,* which gave birth to the psychological, nonmonster, horror movie. Though this led to many adult, serious, fine films, it also eventually led to the slasher-gore films that have currently mutated into today's torture-chic movies, films I find unwatchable. In any event, being monsterless, they lie outside the subject of this look at monster movies, as do the horror-hag pictures that began with the campy delight *Whatever Happened to Baby Jane*.

Hammer continued healthy through the sixties. Christopher Lee was persuaded to put the Dracula cape back on in 1965 for *Dracula Prince of Darkness*, and then couldn't seem to take it off again, continuing to make *Dracula* sequels well into the seventies. As the Hammer formula wore out towards the end of the decade, they began injecting heavier doses of sex, with bare breasts popping out of lesbian vampire's bodices in films like *Lust for a Vampire*, *Twins of Evil*, and *Countess Dracula*.

In 1974, two diametrically opposed takes on *Frankenstein* came out: Paul Morrissey's *Flesh for Frankenstein*, released in America as *Andy Warhol's Frankenstein*, was a 3-D gorefest spoof, full of sex, incest, homosexuality, and internal organs thrust in our faces, all set off by the execrable acting Morrissey's films are generally filled with.

That same year, Mel Brooks's *Young Frankenstein*, which aped and parodied the James Whale films, and took much of its story from *Son of Frankenstein*, became, deservedly, one of the most popular and cherished comedies of all time. I spent a day on the set, observing filming, and, at a preview screening, ventured the opinion to Mel Brooks that it was the best *Frankenstein* movie since James Whale stopped making them, an opinion I still hold. A Broadway musical stage adaptation of *Young Frankenstein*, with Roger Bart and Megan Mulally, is in rehearsal as I write, and will be opening on Broadway in Fall 2007.

In 1975, *The Rocky Horror Picture Show* took all the

transgender impulses running underneath *Franken-stein,* and paraded them across the screen, singing and dancing in fishnet stockings. Initially a failure, it became a midnight-movie hypersuccess, and is now one of the most familiar movie texts ever. Oddly, although the original play fed off the Universal movies, the film version took Hammer for its satiric target. In fact, the same building used for the exteriors of Dr. Frank N. Furter's mad castle was used for the exteriors of Peter Cushing's mad castle back in *Curse of Frankenstein.*

Dracula came back in 1974 as well, in *Blood For Dracula,* a.k.a. *Andy Warhol's Dracula.* Not in 3-D, and slightly wittier than *Flesh for Frankenstein,* it still features dreadful performances from Udo Kier as Dracula, and from Joe Dallesandro. It does include a lot of explicit sex and often-lovely exposed flesh. Dallesandro can not act, but he looked *great* naked. In the wake of the success of *Young Frankenstein* came the much less amusing *Love at First Bite,* with George Hamilton as Dracula. Much later, Mel Brooks turned his hand to spoofing the legend, miscasting Leslie Nielson as the count in the tedious *Dracula Dead and Loving It.*

Following a successful Broadway revival of the same *Dracula* stage play Lugosi had appeared in, Frank Langella brought his smoldering, sexy Dracula to the screen in 1979, in a nonspoofy treatment with Laurence Olivier as Van Helsing. Well-intentioned and lavishly mounted, it's nonetheless a bit of a mess.

Francis Ford Coppola directed the mistitled *Bram Stoker's Dracula* with Gary Oldman as the count. (Full disclosure: I read for a role in this film, and was not cast, so the cynical might assume I have an ax to grind.

Moi?) The closest adaptation of the novel ever, nonetheless, it turned Stoker's demonic villain into a lonely hero, and turned his virginal heroine, Mina, into a slut who can't wait to cheat on her husband with Dracula. Gorgeously mounted, brilliantly designed, it features a bizarre range of talent, from the great Oldman and Anthony Hopkins as Van Helsing, to inept amateur performances from the talent-challenged Keanu Reeves and Wynona Rider. Watching Gary Oldman play scenes with Keanu, one gets the feeling of what one would have seen if Laurence Olivier at the height of his powers had consented to appear in a high school play.

Coppola produced the equally mistitled *Mary Shelley's Frankenstein,* which Kenneth Branagh directed as well as starred in as Victor Frankenstein. His monster was created when he put the brain of John Cleese into the body of Robert DeNiro, which anybody would know is a bad idea on all levels. Faithful to the novel until the climax, it goes spectacularly off the rails once the Monster kills Elizabeth by ripping her heart out of her chest. Then Victor decides to re-animate his bride. She needs a new heart, but instead of a heart transplant, he opts for a *head* transplant, sewing her head onto the body of an unfinished female creature he'd been making. When revived, she is confronted by the handsome, hunky man she's married to, and the repulsive monstrosity who just literally ripped out her heart, both offering themselves as her lover, *and she can't make up her mind!* It's not a difficult choice, but she can't deal with it, and burns the house down instead.

Like *Flesh for Frankenstein,* it's an ugly-looking, repulsive film, despite Branagh running around shirtless a good deal. But while *Flesh for Frankenstein* featured bad acting from bad actors, *Mary Shelley's Frankenstein* features bad acting from *great* actors. They have no excuse for this mess.

Some Baby-Boomers growing up on these movies grew up to become filmmakers that honored them in their work. Joe Danté made the best werewolf movie ever with *The Howling,* and filled his cast with folks from horrors past like John Carradine and Kenneth Tobey, while many of the characters bore the names of directors of classic werewolf movies. Danté included Christopher Lee in the cast of his *Gremlins 2, the New Batch,* and his *Matinee* is a loving tribute to William Castle.

Tim Burton parlayed his boyhood Vincent Price obsession into a short animated film, *Vincent,* and gave Price one last hurrah in *Edward Scissorhands.* More recently, he's seemed intent on reviving Hammer Films, by casting Hammer stalwarts Christopher Lee and Michael Gough in his films. Indeed, his *Sleepy Hollow* seems like the best film Hammer never made. As I write, Burton is shooting *Sweeney Todd, the Demon Barber of Fleet Street,* the great Stephen Sondheim horror musical.

In 1999, Stephen Sommers directed a "remake" of *The Mummy* for Universal. The movie, starring *Gods and Monsters*'s Brendan Fraser, was a gigantic hit. Undeniably entertaining, it was about as far from Karl Freund's moody, atmospheric chiller as you could get, being basically *Indiana Jones Meets Imhotep.* Sommer's subsequent attempts to revive the classic monsters as action movies, *The Mummy Returns* and *Van Helsing,* have been increasingly poor. *Van Helsing*, particularly, with its recasting Stoker's elderly Dutch professor as a Vatican-employed, 007-type, ultrahunky vampire hunter, and pitting him against Dracula, Frankenstein's Monster, and a Wolfman, seemed more a remake of *House of Frankenstein* as a frantic theme-park roller coaster. It's a ghastly mess. Action movies are not the way to bring back the gothic monsters.

But if horror movies are in sad shape today, the monsters can not die. They will be back, and future classic monster movies lie ahead.

But I can hear the cock crow now. The sky is lightening in the east. It's time for me to repair to my crypt, and close the lid on my bed until another day. Thank you for sharing this journey with me. And quoth the Monsters, "Nevermore."